Raising Chickens
for Beginners

The Complete Guide to
Breeds · Housing · Facilities · Feeding
Health Care · Breeding · Eggs · Meat

Max Barnes

Your Free Gift

I'd like to offer you a gift as a way of saying thank you for purchasing this book. It's the eBook called 10 Chicken Coop Plans. There are a lot of free chicken coop plans on the internet; however, not all of them are good enough to follow. I chose 10 of the best-looking, easiest-to-build, or the cheapest chicken coop plans available that you can realistically build in your backyard. You can get your free eBook by scanning the QR code below with your phone and joining our community. Alternatively, please send me an email to maxbarnesbooks@gmail.com and I will send you the free book.

SPECIAL BONUS!
Want this book for free?

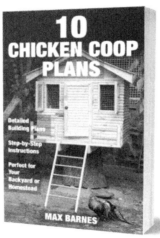

Get FREE unlimited access to it and all of
my new books by joining our community!

**Scan with
your camera
to join!**

Chicken Record Keeping Log Book

Keeping detailed records of your flock is important and I highly recommend all new chicken owners do that. Keeping records of your chickens helps keep things organized and will help you take better care of your flock. I have created a Chicken Record Keeping Log Book that will allow you to keep all the important information about your flock in one convenient place. If you're interested in getting a log book, please scan the QR code below with your phone to find out more. Alternatively, please send me an email to maxbarnesbooks@gmail.com and I will send you the link to the log book.

Scan with your camera to find out more

Contents

Introduction

Why raise chickens? It's a reasonable question to ask, but if you love eggs or chicken meat, and have the space to raise your own chickens, you'd be crazy not to. Chickens can help you live a sustainable lifestyle. Once you have chickens, you'll never again need to purchase eggs or chicken meat from a shop. They are incredibly versatile—you can have chickens to lay eggs, or for meat production, or both if you choose to. It's incredible having a daily supply of fresh eggs laid for you, or fresh poultry from animals that you know have been raised ethically, given the best food and the best care, with plenty of space. Chicken manure is a fantastic fertilizer for your plants and vegetables. You can also have chickens as pets that are entertaining and amusing with their own distinct personalities.

Many people have a keen interest in raising chickens. My friends and family have often asked me about it, and I've helped a number of them to start raising chickens themselves. Many people are initially unsure of where to start, and thinking about everything one needs to keep chickens can feel overwhelming. People aren't born automatically knowing how to care for chickens, so it's natural to not know everything about them, and sometimes it can be hard to know what information to trust on the Internet. This book is thoroughly researched, as well as based on sound and successful experience, and it will save you hundreds of hours of time trying to do the research yourself, having all the information you need in one convenient place. *Raising Chickens for Beginners* will teach you everything you need to know about keeping chickens for eggs, meat, or breeding chickens. This book is a complete guide to different breeds of chickens, housing, feeding them, their health, and everything you need to know about egg production, or having chickens for meat.

What This Book Will Cover

Chapter 1 will introduce you to the benefits of raising chickens; ways on how to find out whether you're allowed to keep chickens where you live so that you don't waste time, resources, and effort if the laws restrict or forbid owning chickens; as well as precautions you need to take before getting chickens.

Chapter 2 is about getting your chickens, learning about best breeds for eggs and meat, as well as dual-purpose chicken breeds, and choosing the right breed for your needs and the climate you live in. It also covers how and where you can get your chickens, how many you should purchase, and having a rough idea of the costs involved.

Chapter 3 will help you learn everything you need to know about housing your chickens: different housing and run options available, building your own coop vs. buying a pre-made one, and various chicken shelter considerations, including size, location, insulation, ventilation, fencing and much more.

Chapter 4 is all about feeding your chickens. You will discover what chickens eat, how to choose feed for your chickens, what and when to feed them depending on their age and purpose (eggs or meat), and water management.

Chapter 5 focuses on chicken health, you will learn about biosecurity, parasites, signs of healthy and unhealthy chickens, and how to deal with common chicken health problems.

Chapter 6 will look at routine management and will give you a good understanding of the daily, weekly, and monthly activities connected to keeping chickens.

Chapter 7 will help you discover everything you need to know about breeding chickens and raising chicks, including mating your chickens, incubating and hatching eggs, caring for newborn chicks and raising them.

Chapter 8 will cover egg production. You will learn how to identify laying hens, understand why roosters aren't required for eggs (unless you want chicks too), possible reasons why your hens may not be laying eggs, and much more. It also contains information on how to gather, clean, and store eggs; how to check egg quality; and an unusual, but tried and tested technique of preserving eggs, that can keep fresh uncooked eggs, fresh as the day they were laid, for up to 8 months (and possibly as long as 2 years).

Chapter 9 is all about raising chickens for meat. It will cover the best breeds of chickens for meat production, feeding your broilers, common health issues that can occur in broilers, butchering meat chickens, and storing chicken meat safely and under sanitary conditions.

Chapter 10 will look at additional benefits of having chickens, such as putting your chickens to work in the garden, using them for pest control, and using their manure as an amazing fertilizer that will help your plants and vegetables to thrive.

Chapter 11 will help you learn everything you need to know about setting up a business around chickens, choosing your sector, whether that is egg production, meat production, or breeding chickens to sell them. This will give you insight into things you need to consider, such as who your target market will be, the costs involved, what you can hope to make as profit, and how to market/advertise your business.

Why I'm Writing This Book

My name is Max, and I grew up on a farm helping my grandmother Anna raise a variety of animals, including chickens, goats, pigs, cows, sheep, horses, ducks, turkeys, and more. One of my first memories was around chickens, and I liked them because they were incredibly friendly and funny, all with their own distinctive personalities. I enjoyed helping my grandma feed them, clean their coops, feeders, and waterers, and I absolutely adored collecting the eggs, and remember as a child, being so careful as I picked them up and placed them in the basket and carried the basket so carefully back to the farmhouse, so as not to break any of them. The delight of having some of those fresh eggs the next morning as dippy eggs, and dipping bread and butter soldiers into their lovely runny yellow yolks is a memory I will always fondly look back on!

As an adult now, I still keep various animals on my property, including chickens. This allows me to lead a sustainable lifestyle. As a family we have lovely fresh eggs every day, more than we in fact need now, so we give some to our family and friends, and we sell some at a local farmers market and local shop which brings in some more income. Some of our eggs are used in baked goods, which also use other produce from our smallholding. Each day when I tend the chickens, it still has that nostalgic feel to me, bringing back childhood memories of working with my grandmother on her farm.

I learned the basics of farming on my grandmother's farm, which have stood me in good stead as an adult, and I've learned a lot of tips and tricks over the years from experience, sometimes learning things the hard way, and learning from fellow chicken keepers and farmers which is invaluable. I now have a lot of experience in raising chickens, and I wanted to write this book to show people that raising chickens is not as difficult as some people may think, and that the benefits you get from doing so far outweigh the time, money, and effort involved. We adore having chickens and know that we're lucky to have them in our lives, and they have most definitely made a tremendous improvement to our sustainable lifestyle.

This book is for beginners who are new to keeping chickens, and it will help you learn everything you need to know about raising chickens for eggs and meat, setting up a business around chickens, as well as putting your chickens to work in the garden and using their manure as fertilizer. It is not a guide to raising any other animals or birds apart from chickens.

So, let's get started right away and move into Chapter 1, to looking at some of the many benefits of raising chickens, checking whether you're able to keep chickens in the area where you live, and to consider any precautions before embarking on your incredible journey of raising chickens!

Chapter 1: Why Raise Chickens?

This chapter will focus on the many wonderful benefits of raising chickens. It will look at whether you are legally able to keep chickens where you live and how to find out this information. It will also consider precautions to take before you start raising chickens, this includes things you should think about in terms of responsibility, time, and costs because whilst it's incredible fun keeping chickens, it is also something that you need to carefully think about before making that commitment. Chickens are living creatures that need to be well cared for.

Benefits of Raising Chickens

1. Eggs

For me personally, the key benefit of raising chickens is having a supply of fresh eggs. As a family, we eat a lot of eggs in many different ways. Poached on toast or muffins (eggs hollandaise), fried with a cooked breakfast, scrambled, boiled with dippy bread soldiers, cold boiled eggs with salads, or egg-mayonnaise sandwiches. We use them to bake cakes and make quiches and frittatas. We make pancake and Yorkshire Pudding mixes with them. Having this incredible supply of organic eggs is simply egg-cellent!

We know exactly where our eggs have come from. We know that they are truly free range, and that the chickens are not just conforming to the bare minimum requirements in terms of space, but have plenty of room and a lovely smallholding to roam around freely. We know that our chickens are well cared for, with the best food given to them, and they are healthy and loved. The good quality food we provide our chickens results in tasty eggs. Provided you're careful with the eggs when you collect them, you know they're fresh and haven't sat on a shelf, and you don't have to worry about them being broken by the time they are delivered (like you do with online shopping).

2. Generate income

It is possible to earn additional income from having chickens. You may find that you have more eggs than you can possibly consume yourself, you could sell them to neighbors, work-colleagues, or at local shops, or a market. If you decide to use chickens for meat, this is another income stream too. Again, similarly with egg production, if you have reared the chickens yourself, you know they have been fed well and looked after well. You know that there have been no additives given to them, and that your chickens have lived a good life in a spacious environment. You can choose to sell chicken feathers and fertilizer if you don't wish to use this yourself. You can sell your chickens to other farmers too.

3. Sustainability

Having your own chickens will help you live more sustainably. You will likely spend more time outdoors looking after them. The chicken poop will help with compost heaps (you can compost eggshells too), or your vegetable or flower beds, and will help whatever you plant to thrive with nutrient-rich fertilizer. You will probably need to purchase eggs or chicken less from a store, meaning it will reduce fuel emissions from travelling. Chickens may help you bring in income if you have a surplus of eggs or meat which you can sell.

4. Reduce garden pests

Chickens will eat vegetables, grass, grubs, bugs, and other pests, which can keep insects out of your garden. They will eat grasshoppers and snails and other bugs that may cause harm to

your garden, including mosquitos and tics too. Chickens will eat many things, so it is sensible to cordon off bits of your garden that you don't want them to have access to.

5.   Weeding

Chickens are great at pulling up weeds in the garden, we keep our chickens free range, and this allows the chickens to have a great quality of life roaming where they want to, and they in turn help keep the garden looking nice and free of weeds. We do ensure that the garden is super secure with chicken wire fences to prevent predators from attacking the chickens.

6. Fertilizer

Chicken poop is one of the best things you can use to fertilize your garden. When you have chickens, they will produce a lot of poop, but you can put this to good use to provide wonderful nutrients to your soil to grow plants and vegetables. It helps create a wonderfully sustainable lifestyle.

7. Enjoyment

Having pets is satisfying and rewarding. Chickens have their own individual personalities and quirks, just like people do. They are entertaining and humorous animals. Ours, because they're free range, regularly walk into the house or jump on the windowsills. They have also been known to get into the greenhouse. Chickens like to explore and play and will scratch about looking for bugs and seeds.

8. Low maintenance

Chickens don't need to be walked or trained like a dog does. They are mostly quiet, and the key things that you need to do for them are feed them correctly, clean the area adequately, and ensure they have shelter and safety from predators. Once you have set up the coop,  feeders, and waterers, then it is just a case of keeping the coop clean, and checking the health of the birds to make sure they don't have any injuries or diseases, but they're relatively low maintenance. Chickens will need things to do to entertain them, like with any pet, but you can have chicken swings, place cabbage on strings, have different wood stumps for them to climb on, and so on.

9. Family fun

Looking after chickens is a good family activity, and this is how I first learned about them from helping my grandmother as a child. It can be a great way to teach children about responsibilities, tasks, how to care for animals, the importance of cleaning animal enclosures, collecting the eggs, securing the grounds where the chickens are kept, and so on.

10. Reduce kitchen waste

Chickens eat a great many different things, they will happily eat your kitchen scraps, for example, leftover bread crusts, vegetable peelings, or oatmeal. They will consume soft fruit, any nuts, or seeds going to waste.

11. Be a part of a community

There are many people who have small holdings or do some farming in their backyard. You may know neighbors who do this, or work colleagues, or find people online, and it's a great way to be in touch with like-minded individuals. It will make your hobby exciting, and there will be lots of people to help with advice if you experience an issue.

12. Health benefits

When you care for living things such as plants or animals, this really gives a boost to your mental health, improving your mood and reducing stress levels. Because of being outdoors, you'll get more fresh air and be more active from working outside to take care of them. There will be a daily routine, where you feed the chickens, change their water, and collect eggs, and spend time with them checking their health and enjoying their company.

Can I Raise Chickens in My Area?

It can sometimes be difficult to work out whether you are allowed to keep chickens where you live. But it's well worth doing the research before you have bought your chickens, and then have to re-home them. Having chickens isn't something that only people who live in the countryside can do. More and more people have chickens in their backyard in rural and urban areas. But it is worth thoroughly researching and investigating first to ensure you won't have any issues.

My friend bought chickens, and lived in rented accommodation, and was then told she had to re-home them. She has re-homed them to a lovely country estate, where they're well

 looked after, but she was upset to do so. There are many places you can check on the law to find out if you are allowed to keep chickens. Laws are sometimes made at the city and sometimes county level. So, for example, some areas of California would allow you to keep chickens and other places don't.

The list below points out some good places to check:

1. **County Zoning Laws**

Ask your Local Health and Zoning Board or local planning board, county clerk, or animal control representative to see if there are any rules or regulations preventing you from keeping chickens in your area. You can usually find the appropriate contact information on your city's website. The county zoning laws are the most important laws at the county level. Some zoning laws restrict the number of livestock you can keep per acre.

2. **Homeowner's Association or Covenants**

If you have a Homeowner's Association in your neighborhood, check with them. Covenants are rules you need to follow from the property deed, which prohibit activities that could impact the neighborhood, so it is worth checking your house deeds.

3. **Municipal Code/City Code**

Contact any local authorities that regulate what you can do with your property. Some towns may have a 'municipal code' online. It may sometimes be termed a 'city code'.

4. **Livestock Ordinance**

Do an online search for where you live for 'livestock ordinance'. You can also check for livestock regulations.

5. **Questions to Ask**

Ensure that you ask the correct questions, as some places may have restrictions regarding the size of the flock you have, the buildings you keep them in, and how much space (acreage) is needed per animal. Here are the questions you should ask:

- How many birds can you legally keep? Some city laws may just allow 2–3, whereas other city laws may allow 10 or more. You need to give your chickens adequate space and keep their living conditions clean and hygienic. Space wise, usually you should have 3 square foot per chicken in a chicken coop, and 10 square foot of outside space per chicken. If you have more space than this, that's great. The more space chickens have, the less this will lead to disease or feather-picking. Chickens need space to spread their wings, take a dust bath, and spend a little time in the sun.

- Are you allowed to have hens and roosters or just hens? Often roosters are prohibited from being kept within city limits because of their crowing, which is OK in the country, but disturbs people living in a town. Sometimes the law may relate to noise disturbances or nuisance animals.

- Do you have to follow any guidance about where you need to construct the coop?

- Do you need to request permission from neighbors before you start to keep chickens, and if so, what information/documents do you need from them as proof?

- Do you need any permits to keep chickens or build a coop?

- Do you have contact people who could take your chickens if you're no longer in a position to look after them?

- If you're not able to have chickens, then you could join with other chicken enthusiasts to outline the benefits and rally community support, to see if you can change the laws in your area.

- If you are planning to keep chickens for meat, you may need to find out if you are able to slaughter chickens where you live. Chicken slaughter will be linked to city health ordinances, and the slaughter of any animal may be prohibited.

6. Neighbors

I would suggest talking to your neighbors prior to purchasing chickens and letting them know your plans. You can let your neighbors know that chickens are quiet and won't cause any trouble. Some cities have nuisance laws that prevent you from keeping livestock if it offends your neighbors. It's an obvious point to make too, but people can move houses, and whilst your current neighbors may be lovely, you don't know who may move in there in the future.

7. Follow other laws

You need to ensure that you are following all other laws, especially ones that relate to noise, sanitation, and animal welfare.

Chicken Terminology

Chicken Types

Bantam: Miniature chickens, about 1/2 to 1/3 size of a regular chicken

Broiler: A chicken bred for meat

Chick: Newly hatched chicken

Cock: Male chicken that is a year or older

Cockerel: Male chicken that is under a year old

Dual-purpose Breed: Breed of chicken that is raised for both eggs and meat

Hen: Female chicken that is a year or older

Juvenile: A young male or female bird

Layer Breed: Breed of chicken that is raised primarily for egg collection

Ornamental Breed: Breed of chicken that is raised primarily for show or exhibition

Production Breed: Breed of chicken that is raised for high egg production or meat production

Pullet: A young female chicken that is under a year old

Rooster: A male chicken (includes cock and cockerel)

Chicken Housing and Environment

Bedding/Litter: A material used to cover the floor in confined spaces, typically wood shavings or straw

Brooder: A type of heated enclosure for raising chicks

Chicken Tractor: A movable chicken coop lacking a floor allowing access to the earth under it

Chicken Wire: Light wire netting with a hexagonal mesh

Coop: An enclosure where chickens are kept safe and secure

Feeder: The container that holds feed for your chickens so that they can eat it without spreading it all over the floor

Hardware Cloth: A sturdy wire mesh product made of metal or plastic used to keep all sorts of predators and pests out

Nesting Box: A private place for your chickens to lay eggs

Roost: A horizontal bar that chickens perch on

Run: A fenced or enclosed outdoor space for your chickens

Waterer: The container that holds and delivers water for your chickens

Chicken Feed Types

All Flock Feed: A feed specifically formulated for mixed flocks of poultry

Calcium: A mineral supplement necessary for strong egg shells, usually comes in the form of crushed up oyster shells

Crumbles: A form of chicken feed that has been pelleted, and then the pellets broken up

Grit: Crushed rock that helps chickens break down food in the gizzard

Layer Feed: A feed formulated for hens at laying age to support healthy and strong egg production

Oyster Shell: Crushed up oyster shells, a mineral supplement that your chickens eat if they need more calcium in their diet

Pellets: A form of chicken feed where the contents are compressed into small, bite-sized pieces that chickens can swallow whole

Scratch: A mixture of blended and whole unfortified grains and cracked corn

Starter Grower Feed: A feed formulated for growing chicks up to laying age, which is typically 16 weeks for hens

Chicken Anatomy

Comb: A featherless crest at the top of a chicken's head

Crest: The feathers protruding from the top of a chicken's head

Crop: A part of a chicken's digestive system that stores food before it can be fully digested in the gizzard

Gizzard: A hard muscular stomach that grinds a chicken's food

Shaft: The dangly hard thing that the feather grows out of

Spurs: A sharp appendage that can grow on the roosters' legs

Vent/Cloaca: An opening in chickens where waste and eggs are expelled

Wattle: Flesh under the beak of a chicken that is used as a heat regulating mechanism

Chicken Health

Amprolium: Medication used as an aid to prevent and treat coccidiosis and can be found in some medicated chicken feeds

Avian Influenza (Bird Flu): A naturally occurring virus that affects chickens and other species of poultry

Bumblefoot: A bacterial infection and inflammatory reaction on the feet of birds

Coccidiosis: Intestinal disease that occurs when a microscopic parasitic organism attaches itself to the intestinal lining

Dust Bath: Bathing in dirt or other substances to help remove external parasites and groom plumage

Fowl Pox: Viral disease in chickens and other species of poultry that causes lesions on skin (cutaneous form) and can affect respiratory tract and upper GI (diphtheritic form)

Mites: Bugs that live on the skin of chickens

Newcastle Disease: An extremely contagious disease affecting birds, including domestic poultry

Pasty Butt: Describes the condition that occurs when a chick's vent is covered in feces and becomes clogged

Poultry Lice: Insects that live only on chickens and their feathers

Quarantine: Keeping certain chickens separate for a set amount of time, do this if they're sick or new to the flock

Salmonella: Intestinal bacteria that is typically heard about when discussing food poisoning

Wry Neck: Typically seen in chicks causing them to twist their neck, stare upwards, and have trouble standing likely caused by a Vitamin E or selenium deficiency

Chicken Reproduction

Blastoderm: A small white bullseye on the egg yolk indicating a fertile egg

Blastodisc: A small white disc on the egg yolk indicating an infertile egg

Bloom: A thin coating that covers an egg and prevents bacteria from affecting the egg

Broody: A chicken that has decided to sit on and hatch a clutch of eggs

Candle/Candling: Shining a light on the backside of an egg to examine its contents

Clutch: A group of 12 to 15 eggs gathered for hatching

External Pip: During the hatching process, the chick's first small crack or hole in the shell is called the external pip

Incubator: A machine that maintains the perfect temperature and humidity to hatch eggs

Internal Pip: During the hatching process, when the chick breaches the membrane into the air cell of the egg, it is called the internal pip

Precautions to Consider Before Getting Chickens

You do need to have a certain commitment if you decide to raise chickens. Like with caring for any pet, it does take some time, and you need to ensure they're protected with adequate shelter from the elements, have good food and clean water, daily and that they are taken to a vet if they have any health issues. They need activities to keep them entertained. They need cleaning out so that their environment is healthy and hygienic.

Definitely check all the laws/regulations and be 100% certain you are allowed to raise chickens before you purchase them or anything required for raising them. You don't want to waste money, time, and effort.

Ensure you have the space for a henhouse or chicken coop—it needs to have a feeder, water containers, roosting areas, and a nest box for every three hens you have. If you have a coop, it should be big enough for you to stand in and be able to clean out the chicken manure comfortably (see Chapter 3, for more information on housing chickens). You need to be easily able to gather the eggs from it. Henhouses can be a bit smaller, but need to be safe to prevent predators from attacking your chickens.

You need to ensure that you have the money to feed the chickens and look after them well moving forwards. Food prices may vary, but you can expect to pay at least $20 for a 50-pound bag of feed. A typical egg-laying hen eats about a 1/4 pound of feed per day, and obviously the more chickens you have, the faster they'll consume that feed. You will need to build or buy a chicken coop and have a run. You'll need wood, fencing, hardware, chicken wire, and if you don't have DIY skills yourself, you may need to pay someone to construct this for you. It's practical to set aside $1,000 for initial costs when first getting started with chickens.

Hens lay eggs throughout the spring and summer months, and a bit into fall, but they need 12–14 hours of daylight. You should be collecting eggs at least once a day. You need to pick eggs up on time because they can get trampled and cracked by chickens when they go to lay more eggs or they can freeze and crack in the colder months if left for too long.

Every week you will need to remove the chicken manure—think about whether you are prepared to do this before getting chickens.

If you wish to go away on holiday, then you will need someone to look after your chickens as well as you would, so this is something to think about very carefully as reliable people who will look after chickens can be hard to find.

If you want a good supply of eggs, then 4–6 hens should be sufficient. Hens tend to lay two eggs every three days. Chickens will produce most of their eggs in the first two years of their lives, and egg production will slow after this. So, if getting chickens for eggs is your key concern, you may need to replace your chickens with younger ones after a few years. You could go down hatching your own either with the help of a broody hen or using an incubator, but this will be discussed in Chapter 7, and the various things you really need to consider very carefully before going down this route.

We started out with two chickens we called Doris and Dotty, and over the years we now have a flock of twelve. They do have their own funny personalities, and we have a lovely supply of eggs that we share with family, friends, neighbors, and work-colleagues. We have taken in some rescue hens too, who looked straggly and unappealing initially as they had been neglected, but now they are so happy, their feathers have filled out, they love playing in the garden and having the freedom to roam and plenty of good food. We learned lots of good tips and techniques from other chicken owners over the years that we'll share with you in this book so that you have all the information you need at your fingertips, rather than having to learn the hard way.

Key takeaways from this chapter:

1. There are so many benefits to having chickens, including having a supply of fresh eggs, meat, fertilizer, and reducing garden pests. They are low maintenance, and you can generate income from selling eggs, meat, fertilizer, and feathers. Chickens provide family fun, they can help with weeding, they will help you lead a sustainable lifestyle, reduce kitchen waste, allow you to socialize as a part of a chicken community, and give you many health benefits.

2. Thoroughly research laws before buying chickens. Look up county zoning laws, the Homeowners' Association, covenants, municipal/city codes, livestock ordinances, ask lots of important questions, check in with your neighbors, and follow other laws relating to noise, sanitation, and animal welfare.

3. Before buying chickens, make sure you have the space for a coop/henhouse. Consider the cost of chickens, from buying them, to their accommodation, feed, vet bills, and so on. Think about collecting eggs daily, cleaning the coop every week, and

think about who will care for your chickens if you wish to go on holiday or in the event of illness.

The next chapter will look at getting your chickens, from choosing the right breed for you to where to actually purchase them from; whether to choose hatching eggs, chicks, pullets, or adults and the pros and cons of these; how many you should get, how to select them, the approximate costs of starting a flock, and finally transporting your chickens home.

Chapter 2: Getting Your Chickens

When you are considering purchasing chickens, there are hundreds of breeds of chickens that you can choose from. You need to carefully consider the main purpose you're buying them for. Do you want them for eggs, for meat, as pets, or to show the chickens? Each breed has different personality traits and may need a different amount of space. You should check that the chickens are suited for the climate you live in too. It is advisable to always start small and see how things go, rather than taking on too much at once. So, you could start with a small flock of 4–6 chickens.

All chicken breeds can be classified into Purebred, Heritage, Hybrid, and Bantams.

Purebred breeds were developed through careful selection by breeders or small farms or through natural intermingling between wild breeds. Purebred chickens typically have distinct appearance and their names usually come from their place of origin, for instance, Orpington, Leghorn, Andalusian, Dorking, and more. Purebred chickens used to have exceptional egg-laying capabilities; however, due to the tendency to breed for show, modern purebred chickens are not quite as capable egg-layers. For example, Australorps were once known to lay up to 350 eggs per year, but modern Australorps can only lay about 250 eggs per year. Some people prefer purebreds because they have more personality than commercial egg-layers, they live longer and lay for longer, and they are generally more adaptable to different conditions.

Heritage breeds are a type of purebred breeds. The term 'heritage breeds' usually refers to older breeds like Cochin. However, 'heritage' is often used interchangeably with 'purebred' and most people do not differentiate between the two.

Hybrid breeds, also sometimes called commercial layers, are egg-laying machines. These breeds are developed through careful scientific selection and genetic engineering in order to maximize egg-laying traits. They are also docile and don't require a lot of space. However, they don't lay for long, usually only for 2 years or less.

Bantam breeds are miniature chickens. They are typically 1/2 to 1/3 the size of a regular chicken. Their eggs are also about half the size of regular eggs, usually 2 regular eggs equal 3 bantam eggs in recipes. They are a perfect choice if you don't have a lot of space. All purebred chickens have bantam counterparts. There are also true bantams which are bantam only and don't have regular-sized counterparts.

Choosing the Right Breed for You

Choosing the right breed for you depends entirely on what you want your chickens for. Do you want chickens that will produce a lot of eggs for you? Do you want chickens for meat? Do you want friendly chickens as family pets? Or do you want a special looking chicken to show it? Some hens have feathered feet like Faverolles; other hens have cheek muffs and bears, like Ameraucanas; Polish chickens have unusual hairdos.

Polish Chicken

There are many breeds of chickens with wonderful names, including Silkies, Russian Orloffs, Silver-Laced Wyandottes, and many more. A wonderful thing about chickens, is that you don't have to pick just one breed and stick to that, chickens from all different breeds usually get along with one another, and if you have different breeds, it will make the eggs you collect much more varied in color. If you are limited for space, then buying bantams, which are smaller, could be a better option for you.

Climate

It is sensible to select chickens that are suited to the climate in which you live. Many chickens are fine even in colder climates, but some breeds really struggle in the heat, such as Brahma and Chantecler, who prefer cooler climates. If you do live in a very hot climate, you may want to purchase Phoenix or Minorca chickens that do well in such conditions.

Phoenix

A hot climate is typically one where the temperature is above 90°F (32°C). Other Mediterranean breeds that like the warmth include Penedesencas, Leghorns, and Andalusians. These chickens are small, sleek, and have a large comb to help them stay cool.

If you live in a cold climate, then chickens that have larger bodies and a smaller comb would be preferable, such as Wyandottes, Barred Rocks, Cochins, Buff Orpingtons, and Australorps.

Chickens with lots of feathers will do better in colder temperatures because they have a thicker coat. It's best to avoid feathered leg chickens in the cold because mud and slush can stick to their legs, causing frostbite. If you live in a cold climate, you can put Vaseline on the birds' combs and wattles, to help prevent frostbite.

Wyandotte

Egg production

All breeds of chickens produce eggs, but they have different production levels and different egg sizes. Your choice over which hens to purchase may depend on the space you have available, what color eggs you want, the size of eggs you want, and how many eggs you want.

Temperament

If you're purchasing chickens more to be friendly family pets, then Australorps, Buff Orpingtons, or Brahmas are very friendly, they're docile and content chickens. Other breeds with a docile temperament include Silkies, Cochins, and Faverolles. Bantams are a lot smaller than regular-sized chicken breeds, so this could be a good option for a family with small children. If you want a docile chicken, I wouldn't recommend Araucanas. Whilst they lay fantastic olive-green eggs, they can be quite flighty hens.

Australorp

Best Breeds for Eggs

For many people, the main benefit of raising backyard chickens is having a fresh supply of eggs. I still remember walking down to chickens' nesting boxes on my grandmother's farm as a kid and picking up those warm, fresh eggs.

While it may seem fairly obvious, most beginners don't realize that the breed of chicken you get makes a huge impact on the number of eggs you should expect to receive each day.

Some breeds, such as Japanese Bantams, tend not to lay eggs, whereas Hybrid hens can lay more than 280 eggs per year, an egg almost every day.

Choosing the right breed is important if you want a steady supply of fresh eggs all year long, so here are the best egg-laying chicken breeds:

1. Golden Comet

There are many different hybrid breeds, and Golden Comet is one of the most common. Hybrids have been bred to lay huge amounts of eggs whilst only consuming small amounts of food, which makes them cheaper to feed than other breeds.

Eggs

Golden Comet hens typically lay around 280 eggs per year. Their eggs are usually medium-sized and brown in color.

Color

Golden Comets are typically a golden-brown color with soft white tail feathers.

Character

Golden Comets tend to be very tough and resilient chickens and rarely ever become broody. If you are looking for a solid all-year-round egg-layer that is easy to look after, Golden Comet is definitely a great choice for you.

2. Rhode Island Red

Rhode Island Red chickens originated from America and they're known as dual-purpose chickens, which means you can raise them for both eggs and meat. They are known to be great foragers, so they make excellent free-range birds and penned chickens too, as long as you keep moving the pen around for ample forage. They are one of the most popular chicken breeds because they are tough and lay lots of eggs.

Eggs

A Rhode Island Red chicken typically lays 250 eggs a year. Their eggs are medium-sized and brown in color.

---

[1] Image from knowyourchickens.com: https://www.knowyourchickens.com/golden-comet-chicken/

Color

Contrary to their name, Rhode Island Reds actually have brown and black feathers, giving them a dark appearance.

Character

Rhode Island Reds are known for being tough and are more than capable of looking after themselves. They are very friendly and are commonly picked by first-time chicken keepers.

3. Sussex

Just like the Rhode Island Red, the Sussex is a dual-purpose breed, which means you can raise them for eggs and meat.

Eggs

A Sussex hen can easily lay 250 eggs a year. Their eggs will vary in color from brown to creamy white.

Color

The Sussex breed has eight different colors, the most common one being a pure white body with a black neck and tail

feathers.

Character

They are very calm chickens who would happily forage in a garden without destroying it. If you want a tame breed that would eat from your hand, then Sussex is a great choice for you. Be careful when raising Sussex with other breeds though, due to their docile nature, they often get bullied by other more bossy breeds.

4. Leghorn

Leghorns were brought to the US from Italy back in the 1800s and they have been a popular choice for a backyard chicken ever since. White Leghorn chickens are a hardy breed. Although they are better suited for a coop or a pen rather than free range, during the summer months, when it's warm and the forage is readily available, they will also make a fine free-range chicken too.

Eggs

Leghorns can lay around 250 eggs per year. Their eggs are white and medium-sized.

Color

Leghorns are beautiful birds, with a full white body and a large thick red comb.

Character

Whilst Leghorns are a great pick for a beginner, if you're looking to tame your chickens, you might have a problem with Leghorns, as they are known for being shy and hard to tame. They do chicken out easily (pun intended).[2]

---

[2] Image from Chicken Scratch: https://cs-tf.com/leghorn-chicken/

5. Red Sex Link

Red Sex Link is a popular hybrid chicken breed. They are known for their quick growth and high production rate of large brown eggs. Their unique advantage is that they can be sexed by their dominant feather color on the day they hatch, which makes it easy to separate males and females. With Sex Links, you can be confident you're purchasing hens from a hatchery or a breeder.

Eggs

The Red Sex Link are hardy free-range birds, and they usually lay around 250 per year. Their eggs are brown and are medium to large in size.

Color

Red Sex Link are golden brown in color with some white feathers around their necks, tails, and sometimes body.

Character

The Red Sex Links are not known for being aggressive, they're docile chickens and tolerate other birds well. They make great pets because of their overall easy-going disposition, but they are not particularly broody.

3

---

3 Image from cluckin.net: https://cluckin.net/red-sex-linked-chickens-and-how-to-breed-them.html

6. Australorp

Australops are gorgeous chickens, they are friendly, and make great egg-layers. They are a great choice for beginners. They tolerate confinement well, but as other larger breeds they are better suited for the free-range lifestyle. They can be quite difficult to raise with other breeds because they tend to bully other birds and sometimes even eat their eggs.

Eggs

Australorps usually produce around 250 eggs per year. They are light brown in color and medium-sized.

Color

Australoprs are absolutely gorgeous with their black feathers with a beetle-green sheen.

Character

While they are typically not aggressive, they tend to bully other breeds and even eat their eggs sometimes. Keep that in mind if you want to raise them with other birds.

7. Plymouth Rock

The Plymouth Rock (Barred Rock) is a fantastic pick for a beginner chicken keeper. They are one of the sweetest and most friendly chickens, and they get along well with other birds. They are also great foragers and pretty good egg-layers.

Eggs

A Plymouth Rock usually lays around 200 eggs a year. Their eggs are light brown in color and small to medium in size.

Color

They are typically grey, with white stripes wrapping around their body.

Character

They are large birds that are well suited to the free-range lifestyle.

Just like the Sussex, they are sweet and friendly birds who can easily be tamed.

8. Golden Laced Wyandotte

These big birds are gorgeous and many people buy them for looks alone. But looks are not the only thing they've got going for them. They are good egg-layers, terrific foragers, and they are gentle and calm. [4]

Eggs

Golden Laced Wyandottes usually lay around 200 eggs a year. Their eggs are medium to large in size and light brown in color.

---

[4] Image from Pinterest: https://www.pinterest.co.uk/pin/173670129367156771/

Color

The background color is dark brown or black and they have golden lacing all over their bodies.

Character

They are quiet and reserved, but at the same time, they're very active and make great foragers which makes them great free-range chickens.

9. New Hampshire Red

New Hampshire Reds were developed in New Hampshire and Massachusetts as a separate strain of Rhode Island Red breed. They are hardy and broody and New Hampshire Red hens are great mothers.

Eggs

New Hampshire Reds typically lay around 200 eggs per year. They are light brown in color and medium-sized.

Color

New Hampshire Reds look quite similar to Rhode Island Reds, but their feathers are a lighter shade of red.

Character

They tend to get quite broody and are good setters. They make excellent mothers too. They are friendly birds and can make great pets.

5

---

5 Image from Insteading: https://insteading.com/chickens/breeds/new-hampshire/

10. Buff Orpington

Buff Orpington chickens originate from Kent, England, and they make great backyard chickens. They are big and beautiful birds that also make great pets. They are not the most prolific egg-layers, but they make up for it with their incredibly docile nature.

Eggs

Buff Orpingtons typically lay around 180 eggs a year.

6

Color

They are a gorgeous golden-yellow color and have a really thick layer of feathers.

Character

Buff Orpingtons are one of the most docile breeds and they make a great garden pet. You can train them to eat from your hand and socialize with you quite easily.

Bantam Chickens

Bantam chickens are miniature chickens. Bantams are not a breed, the term 'Bantam' refers to the size of the chicken, and there is a variety of different Bantam breeds. All purebred chickens have bantam counterparts. There are different types of Bantams, such as True Bantams, Miniaturized Bantams, and Developed Bantams.

True bantams have developed naturally without humans. They do not have regular-sized counterparts and are naturally small. Some examples of true bantams are the Rosecombs and Sebrights.

---

6 Image from Chicken And More: https://www.chickensandmore.com/buff-orpington/

Miniaturized bantams have been developed by humans from existing regular-sized breeds, such as Rhode Island Reds, Orpingtons, and more.

Developed bantams have been selectively bred from already small chickens to create different bantam varieties. Examples of developed bantams include Japanese, Pekin, Cochin, and more.

Bantams are typically 1/2 to 1/3 of the size of a regular chicken, so they can be a great choice if you have limited space, but still want to raise chickens. Their eggs are usually half the size of regular-sized chickens' eggs. Typically, 3 bantam eggs are equal to 2 regular eggs in cooking. Naturally, they eat less than regular chickens and require less space. While a regular chicken needs at least 3 sq. ft. of space, 2 sq. ft. is plenty for a bantam.

They do not require any special care compared to regular chickens. However, since they are smaller, their metabolic is faster, so they tend to feel colder and don't do well in colder climates. You can use a chicken coop heater to keep them warm. They also can fly better than regular chickens, so even though they are smaller, you'll need slightly higher fencing—usually a foot taller than for regular chickens. You can consider clipping their wings if they keep flying out of their run. You can keep bantams with regular-sized chickens; however, I don't recommend it. They tend to get bullied by bigger chickens due to their size.

It's highly likely you'd want bantams for eggs, so if that's the case, you should avoid Japanese, Pekin, and Sebright breeds, as they only lay 50–80 eggs per year. Easter Eggers and Araucanas are among the best egg-laying bantam breeds and can lay up to 280–300 eggs per year. Brahmas and Cochins are proficient egg-layers too, and can lay over 200 eggs per year.

Best Breeds for Meat

There has been a move away from eating commercially grown chickens, which may sometimes have been given growth hormones, to raising one's own chickens for meat. There are breeds of chicken that produce more meat than others. When you raise your own chickens for meat, you know that their feed has been natural, without hormone injections. Chickens produced for meat are called 'Broilers'. These chickens tend to grow faster in comparison to egg-laying chickens. Usually by the time they are 10 weeks old, they weigh 10 lb, which is enough to feed a family. There are different breeds you can purchase, here are some of the most popular breeds:

1. Cornish Cross

Cornish Cross is a very common chicken to buy for meat and is what commercial meat raisers tend to use. They weigh between 8 and 12 lb and grow in 4–6 weeks. They have an excellent growth rate, the only downside is that they eat quite a lot to reach that weight. They

have broad breasts and large thighs. Cornish Cross and their associated hybrids are extremely favored when it comes to raising your own chickens for meat purposes. They grow faster and taste better than dual-purpose chicken breeds.

[7]

---

[7] Image from Backyard Chickens: https://www.backyardchickens.com/reviews/cornish-cross.10897/

2. Bresse

These chickens are much smaller and don't produce as much meat, but they have a lovely taste and their meat is exceptionally tender. In fact, the Bresse is famous for being the best meat tasting chickens in the world and also for their tenderness. They take 16–20 weeks to grow. They will only

weigh 5–7 lb though. The only drawback is their cost, as they are not as popular in the US as in Europe, especially France. With that said, once you have your chickens and breeding pairs, the only expense you will have is the food necessary to raise them.[8]

3. Jersey Giants

They were developed in the US with the aim of replacing classic turkey. This didn't happen, but this breed earned a place of its own in the poultry world.

As the name suggests, these birds are huge, they weigh between 11 and 13 lb, and their size can appeal to people. They grow to this size typically in 16–21 weeks. They grow slower than some other breeds, but you will get more meat from them. While they take longer to grow, they also lay

---

[8] Image from The Happy Chicken Coop: https://www.thehappychickencoop.com/bresse-chicken/

extra-large brown eggs, so you can use them as egg-laying hens while your wait for them to reach their peak weight.

4. Freedom Rangers

Freedom Rangers were developed with the aim to be good pasture-fed meat chickens. They need a lot of space and low protein feeds, and they prefer to roam around in a large pen.

They are versatile eaters and are better at food scouting than Cornish Crosses. They love eating field bugs and corn feed. They will grow within 9–11 weeks and they typically weigh 5–6 lb. While they are not the largest chickens and take a bit longer to grow, many people love them for their taste. Some say they're best for rotisserie oven.[9]

---

[9] Image from Voodoo Chicken Farm: https://voodoochickenfarm.com/freedom-rangers/

Dual-Purpose Breeds

You can buy dual-purpose chickens, which allow you to collect the eggs from the chickens, while you wait for them to grow into meat. Breeds that fit this category include:

1. White Leghorn

White Leghorns are one of the best egg-layers—they can lay around 280 eggs per year. They weigh 5–6 lb and they need 16–21 weeks to reach that weight. They are active foragers and are known to be quite friendly, which makes White Leghorns a fantastic dual-purpose breed for beginners.

10

11

2. Wyandottes

Wyandottes are a larger breed and they are decent egg-layers too. They have a gorgeous coloring with solid feathers laced with contrasting colors. They are a friendly, docile breed. They weigh around 8 lb and take about 16–18 weeks to reach that weight. They lay about 200 eggs per year.

---

[10] Image from Chicken Scratch: https://cs-tf.com/leghorn-chicken/
[11] Image from Roy's Farm: https://www.roysfarm.com/wyandotte-chicken-farming/

3. Rhode Island Red

Rhode Island Reds are fantastic egg-layers, but they make a great meat chicken too. They are a bit more aggressive than some other breeds, but it's nothing too serious. They are a hardy breed and do well in either a free-range or a confined environment. Rhode Island Reds weigh 6–8 lb and take 20–22 weeks to reach that weight. They lay around 250 eggs per year.

4. Sussex

This is a popular type of dual-purpose chicken and a perfect breed for beginners. They are one of the heaviest layers, literally. Not only because they lay around 250 eggs per year, but they also weigh around 8 lb on average. It usually takes them 20–22 weeks to grow to that weight. Despite their size, Sussex chickens don't need big spaces. They are a calm breed and a perfect pick for beginners.

5. Chantecler

If you live in a cold climate, Chantecler is perfect for producing eggs and meat. These birds thrive in cold climates. They can lay up to 200 large brown eggs per year. They are very docile and they grow rather quickly too. They weigh 7–9 lb and it takes them 11–16 weeks to fully grow. They like to forage, so they make great free-range birds.

Options to Get Your Chickens

When you're first starting out keeping chickens, it can be hard to know whether you should buy eggs, or chicks, or adult chickens. The sections below will discuss the pros and cons of the available options and will help you make an informed decision on this.

Hatching Eggs

When you purchase eggs, you will need to buy an incubator, which will incubate the eggs usually for 21 days at the right temperature and humidity. You will need to monitor the temperature and humidity and adjust accordingly and turn the eggs. Likely not all eggs will hatch, but seeing the ones that do is a really wonderful experience. If you are completely new to chickens, it's probably best not to start out with hatching them, as there is an art to it. Incubating eggs is covered in Chapter 7. It may be best to purchase chicks if you're a beginner—see the next paragraph.

Chicks

You can purchase chicks that are just a day old. When you buy chicks, it's easy to develop a bond with them when you feed, teach, and pet them. It's lovely to see them grow into bigger chickens that strut around your backyard. Chicks require care in their first few weeks of life, and we'll discuss raising chicks in Chapter 7.

You'll need to keep the chicks warm with a heat lamp and line the brooder they're in with things like pine shavings and newspapers. If you are purchasing chicks, there are some things to be prepared for. Do ensure you have everything in place before the chicks arrive because sometimes the delivery can come a day or two early.

Also, as upsetting and unpleasant as this sounds, sometimes a chick or two may die during delivery, so be especially careful if this is new to you, and perhaps don't open newly delivered chicks in front of children. Most hatcheries offer replacements or refunds, but it's not the financial aspect, as much as the upset of a living creature not making it. If you are buying through this method, you could always order a few more than you need to ensure that you have the flock size you want.

You can buy straight run chicks, meaning that they are not sexed and you will get a mix or males and females; or sexed chicks if you want only females for laying eggs. Even when you purchase chicks that have been sexed, you can still get a male, as sexing is not error-proof. If you've purchased sexed chicks and some of them turned out to be males, most stores will offer a refund, but won't take the rooster back. Some farm or farm stores may buy back roosters. Refund and return policies differ from one place to another, so make sure to research that before purchasing chickens from a particular place.

Here are the pros and cons of buying chicks to start a flock:

Pros

- Buying chicks gives you the ability to bond with them and helps chicks start socializing with people from a very young age
- Chicks have a very low risk of carrying diseases from environmental exposure
- Chicks don't have any habits or ingrained behavioral problems
- Vaccinations for Marek's disease are available
- Much less expensive to purchase than pullets

Cons

- While chicks are less expensive to purchase than pullets initially, the total cost of getting them to the point of lay can be more expensive than buying pullets

- They require special care for about 8 weeks once you get them

- You'll have to wait for them to grow and mature before they start laying eggs

- There is always a risk of buying a male chicken even with sexed chicks

Pullets

This is the name for a chicken that is under a year old and has been laying eggs for just a few months. Their eggs initially may be smaller than what you are used to until they get into egg laying. Buying pullets can be more expensive than buying young chicks initially; however, it is usually cheaper than growing chicks until they get to the point of lay.

Here are the pros and cons of buying pullets:

Pros

- There is little to no wait to start laying eggs

- Almost no risk of buying a male chicken

Cons

- You won't have the ability to bond and socialize with your chicken from an early age

- They may have some unwanted ingrained habits and behaviors

- There is always a risk of getting scammed and being sold older, less productive chickens

- There is a risk of carrying diseases from environmental exposure

- They are more expensive to purchase than chicks, but keep in mind that bringing chicks to the point of lay can be more expensive than just buying pullets

Adults

If you don't want to wait for six months for chicks to grow, then you can buy older chickens that are ready to start laying eggs. Chicks can take a lot of care and are vulnerable, whereas adult hens are less time-consuming. You will require a coop or henhouse for them. The main disadvantage of buying adult chickens is that it's very difficult to tell their age. Adult chickens are usually very productive egg-layers for two years, but this lessens as they get older. If you are buying older chickens, you don't really know what condition they have lived in, in terms of feed and cleanliness for the first six months of their life. If you want adult hens, you could look at animal shelters or rescue sanctuaries.

Pros

- They will lay eggs right away
- No risk of buying a male chicken
- You can find good deals or sometimes adopt chickens from animal shelters or rescue sanctuaries

Cons

- You won't have the ability to bond and socialize with your chicken from an early age
- They may have some unwanted ingrained habits and behaviors
- It's very difficult to tell the age of chickens, you will have to take the seller's word for it
- There is a risk of carrying diseases from environmental exposure

Places to Buy Chickens

Hatcheries

You can order day-old chicks online or via phone from hatcheries and choose which breeds you want to add to your flock of chickens. They usually offer chicks from February to

April, and sometimes even later, into spring and summer. Most hatcheries have an extensive breed selection, and some accept orders in advance.

You can do an online search for hatcheries near you, it's best to choose one that is the closest to you so that the babies aren't travelling long to get to you. Hatcheries can post chicks to you. In the summer they will post a few, but in the winter they post larger orders because chicks need to keep each other warm during shipping. Sometimes hatcheries offer a pick up option, so you can pick your chicks up from the store and transport them safely to your home.

Feed Stores

Feed stores, such as Tractor Supply Company, may also sell hatching eggs or day-old chicks. Like hatcheries, they usually offer chicks from February to April. Feed Stores typically offer great prices and you can choose your chicks in store. The breed selection is often limited and most feed stores have minimum purchase requirements of 4–6 chicks at a time. You can find someone else who is willing to purchase chicks and split the order.

Local Farmers

Local farmers will sell hatching eggs, or day-old chicks, or adult chickens. There may only be certain breeds available, and they may not know the gender. At a farmers' market, even if people themselves don't sell chickens, they may have a friend who breeds them.

Swap Meets

Sometimes at Easter people buy chicks because they think of the Easter bunny and Easter eggs, but then they haven't thought through the care and attention that the chicks need. Sometimes you can buy these from them, or they will give them away to a good home. Other times, people may be moving and selling their flock, or have outgrown their hobby.

How Many to Buy?

If you're buying eggs to hatch, you should consider the fact that there is the chance that they may not hatch, so you may want to buy a few more than you expect. But, as a beginner, chicks may be the better option.

If you're buying chickens because you want eggs, think about how many eggs you typically use in a week. One hen may produce 4–5 eggs in a week. Perhaps add a couple more, just in case some of your chickens become sick or injured. So, if you want 16 eggs per week, then you could get 6 hens. Four hens would typically produce this amount, but you can have 2 more, as a backup.

Hens do not need a rooster in order to lay eggs, this is a common misconception. If you don't have a rooster in your flock, your hens' eggs simply won't be fertilized and will never turn into chicks. There are certain benefits to having a rooster in your flock, as well as some drawbacks. First of all, check the local laws in order to find out whether you're allowed to have a rooster at all. They will crow, so some places forbid having a rooster, as they are considered to be 'nuisance animals'. If you'd like to keep multiple roosters, I would recommend keeping 1 rooster for every 10 hens. This ratio can differ from breed to breed. More active breeds, such as Leghorns, can have a higher hen to rooster of 1:12 because of their higher energy. While more mellow breeds, such as Orpingtons, can have a lower ratio of 1:6. In my experience, the 1:10 ratio has always worked fine and it's a great starting point. If you have too many roosters in your flock, they will fight each other to assert dominance, and the dominant rooster will do everything he can to prevent other roosters from mating with his hens.

In case you're allowed to have a rooster and considering getting one, here are some pros and cons of having a rooster in your flock.

Roosters' main mission is to protect his flock. They watch out for predators, and if they notice one, they will alert the hens to run for cover, while the rooster will fight the predator. I've heard a lot of stories from people who got tired of their roosters' shenanigans, and got rid of them, only to find their flock destroyed by a predator a few days later. If you know there are lots of predators in your area, and you can keep a rooster, it can be a great idea to have one in your flock.

Roosters are great flock managers and will keep hens at ease, which can help them lay more and better-quality eggs. Not only do roosters protect their flocks from predators, but they also stop petty hen squabbles, they make sure hens are fed and watered, and they find treats for them.

It's quite an obvious point to make, but having a rooster will allow you to hatch chicks. Roosters will mate with hens and fertilize their eggs. Eggs can be incubated by a broody hen or using an incubator. You can still gather and eat fertilized eggs, they don't differ in taste or nutritional value from unfertilized eggs, and you won't accidentally find a chick inside, as they need incubating for at least 21 days in order to hatch.

With that said, roosters can be very active and mate with hens quite often, an average rooster can mate up to 30 times a day. Which, of course, takes a toll on your hens. Hens lose feathers from mating when a rooster mounts them. So, it can be a good idea to separate them for a few days once in a while.

Roosters can be quite noisy. Contrary to popular belief, they don't just crow once in the morning. It can be fine if you live in the countryside and don't mind hearing your rooster crowing occasionally. But if you have neighbors, it's highly likely they won't appreciate that.

Roosters can be quite nasty and aggressive. They protect their flock from predators, but from their point of view, predators also come with 2 legs, and the fact you're feeding them doesn't bother roosters too much. They have 'spurs' on the back of their legs which are very good at ripping flesh, and they bite really hard for an animal that doesn't have teeth. They can also be nasty to chicks, and can even kill them if a hen pays a chick too much attention to consider time for mating. However, not all roosters are nasty. You can check the list of breeds to see which breeds have more mellow temperament.

How to Pick Your Chickens

When you are picking chicks, pullets, or adults, there are signs of healthy and unhealthy chickens that you should be aware of.

Here are the things you should look out for:

- A healthy hen should have clear, bright eyes without any discharge. Cloudy eyes or lack of alertness usually signify blindness or underlying disease.

- They should be alert and active and naturally be curious about their environment and you.

- Their feathers should be clean and have a nice bright color. There should not be any bald patches or injuries.

- When you pick up a chicken, you should feel nice plump weight. If you can the breast bone, it's highly likely the chicken is malnourished and underweight.

- Check the beak to make sure it's not broken or flaking off. It should be straight and not twisted or crossed. A damaged beak will not always grow back, and chickens with broken beaks will have problems eating and drinking.

- Check the vent to see if it's clear. Loose stools can accumulate around the vent and seal it. Pasted vent can be fatal if left untreated.

- Check the legs to see that they're straight and not too scaly. If they are scaly, it can mean an infestation of scaly leg mites. Below is an example of how healthy chicken legs should look like.

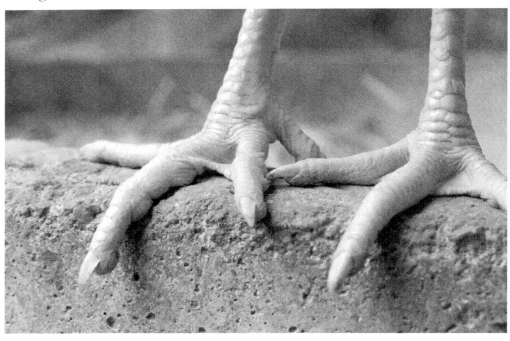

Approximate Costs of Starting a Flock

It is definitely sensible to think carefully about how much your chickens will cost you prior to getting them, and always consider added extras of things that you hadn't anticipated, such as extra fencing, extra waterers, vet bills and healthcare for them.

The prices given here are for 5 chickens. Adapt these prices accordingly, depending on how many chickens you have in your flock.

If you feed your chickens regular feed, then that will typically be around $30 per month. But, if you opt for non-GMO feed, this can be up to $150 per month, which clearly is a big difference. You might want to cost for treats like black soldier fly larvae or treats that contain mealworms, bee pollen, and rose petals. The better food you feed your chickens, the more eggs they'll lay, and the better quality they'll be. Chickens generally need each ½–1 cup or around a ¼ pound of feed per day. You may also want to provide herbal supplements, like nesting herbs, to keep them and their immune system healthy. These herbs vary, but can often include things like chamomile, lavender, calendula, spearmint, dill, roses, and fenugreek.

You could expect 5 chickens, over 5 years, on average, considering the coop, feed, bedding, other costs, and the birds themselves, to cost you approximately $70 a month. These costs don't consider the things that can save or make you money, such as you no longer needing to purchase eggs from a shop, or selling eggs, meat, chickens themselves, manure, or feathers. So, you could reduce these costs, or even make a profit.

Chicken coops vary in price, you can buy one for approximately $300, but this may not be that sturdy and may need replacing after a couple of years. You may be able to build your own if you're good with DIY and have spare wood lying around; or you could pay up to $2,000 for a handmade chicken coop. So, really investigate the type of coop you want and factor this into your costs before purchasing chickens, as the coop is usually the biggest initial expense when you're starting a backyard flock. Purchasing a garden shed to turn into a coop can be a good idea because you could convert it back into a shed if you decide in the future you no longer wish to keep chickens.

Bedding will typically cost around $20 per month. Usually, feeders and waterers cost around $5. It can always be worth having a few spares just to ensure your chickens all have a good chance to get food and water, and in case any break. Baby chicks are usually around $5 each for most breeds (females tend to be more expensive than males). It also does depend on the breed, and whether the breed is rare. Adult chickens vary in price and can be between $1 up to $30. Pullets, young female chickens ready to lay, typically cost between $15 and $25. Some breeds of chickens are super expensive, such as the all-black chicken Ayam Cemani, which can cost $5,000.

Bringing Your Chickens Home

If you have purchased chicks, you will need a brooding box for them. The box needs to have sides high enough to stop the chicks from escaping and needs a food and water dish. It needs to be draft proof because chicks are very sensitive to cold drafts. It should be filled with pine shavings and paper towels or newspaper to help the chicks stand. Chicks do need warmth so they will require a heat lamp or electric hen heat plate. They'll need to be warmed until they are 6–7 weeks old. You can start the temperature at 95°F and reduce this by 5 degrees each week until the ambient temperature is reached. If they huddle together, they are too cold. If they are spread around the edges, they may be too hot. If you are keeping a brooding box full of chicks in the house, do ensure that any other pets, such as cats and dogs, can't get to them. If you have

children who are likely to leave doors open, perhaps put a hook catch on a door high up out of their reach so that the door can't be pushed open, letting other pets in. Baby chicks will kick up dust and have dander, so if you or someone else in the house has allergies, keep them out of bedrooms, dining, and kitchen areas.

If you are keeping chicks in an outbuilding, you really need to ensure it is predator-proof. Typical predators can include foxes, weasels, raccoons, and many other carnivorous creatures. Once chickens are allowed outside, once again, the area needs to be predator-proof, including birds of prey, such as hawks and owls.

After Doris and Dotty, when we moved to a slightly bigger house that had a larger garden, our first serious chicken purchase was of a dozen Rhode Island Reds. They are very docile chickens, not very noisy, they are incredible egg-layers, so we were inundated with delicious eggs. I usually collected around 8–9 eggs a day when they were laying. Rhode Island Reds do well in cold and warm climates, they're very versatile.

Key takeaways from this chapter:

1. Decide on the reasons for wanting chickens so that you can choose a breed best suited for your needs.

2. Consider correct breeds of chickens for the climate you live in.

3. There are specific breeds for eggs, depending on how many eggs you want per month, plus the size of them and their color.

4. Choosing chickens for meat will depend on what size you want, their taste, and how long you want them to take to grow.

5. When you buy chickens, you have a choice of buying eggs and incubating them until they hatch, or buying chicks, pullets, or adults.

6. You can buy chickens from hatcheries, local farms, chicken breeders, swap meets, and feed stores.

7. You could start small, with 4–6 hens, and build your flock gradually.

8. Healthy chickens should have clear, bright eyes, straight legs and beaks, be active and curious, and have clear bright feathers.

9. An approximate cost for 5 chickens over 5 years would work out at around $70 per month, including the coop.

The next chapter will cover the housing for chickens, looking at the many different housing options you can choose from. It will cover various considerations for a chicken coop, such as size, location, insulation and ventilation, storage spaces, nesting boxes, lighting, electricity, and more. This chapter considers whether it's best to buy or build your own chicken coop. It will cover runs and yards for chickens and how to make them safe. And finally, it will discuss fencing to keep chickens out of parts of the garden that you don't want them to venture into and to keep predators out to ensure your chickens are safe and won't be injured or killed.

Chapter 3: Housing for Your Chickens

Once you've decided to raise chickens and have checked you're legally allowed to keep them where you live, you should decide on the type of chicken you want for a specific purpose. With that purpose in mind, you'll then have to choose the breeds you want, and where you'll purchase them from. You then need to think about what housing you will place your chickens in once you get them home. This chapter will look at the different chicken housing options you have available to you, chicken shelter considerations you need to consider, and whether you should buy or build your own coop. This chapter will end by looking at runs and yards for chickens, and the all-important fencing to keep your chickens safe, and protect your garden from chickens so that they don't eat plants and scratch up soil.

When you get your housing right for your chickens, this goes a long way to ensuring you have healthy and happy chickens. Chickens need a house where they can eat, have a lovely dust bath, sleep peacefully in safety, and be comfortable without disturbing others. Chickens will have a longer lifespan and be happier when they have a consistent housing that is private and clean, and they'll lay their eggs there. Chickens will want somewhere that is secure where they can go when the sun sets, and where they can sleep until morning. The housing should keep them warm and dry and be well ventilated. By having the chickens in a chicken coop, this helps keep the chicken droppings in a central place, which makes them easier to clean. Whilst a chicken coop may

be initially an expensive investment, it is a one-off cost that once you have will last for years.

It can be ideal if you can arrange everything that chickens need within their space, such as storage for their food and a large home for them to stay in. When you're preparing a chicken coop, there are 7 key things that you need to consider:

1. It needs to withstand all types of weather
2. It must be spacious for your chickens
3. It needs ventilation to keep your chickens healthy
4. It must contain nesting boxes
5. You need to have roosts fitted
6. There should be an outside roaming pen area for the birds to stretch their legs, wings, and get good fresh air, take dust baths, eat insects, and so on
7. The coop must be safe and secure to prevent any predators from getting in

Chicken Housing Options

There are many different chicken housing options and deciding which is perfect for your chickens can be tricky, but the information below should help.

Free Range

Free-range chickens can go where they please and make good use of space. Chickens raised free range lay healthier eggs. They can interact with other chickens in a social way and not be too confined. They can gather their diet as they graze the garden space. They don't tend to have any problems with mites and lice that more enclosed chickens can. You won't have to do as much cleaning if the chickens are free range. Chickens can help keep garden pests in check and prevent the pests from eating your plants. You will need to ensure that your garden is as protected from predators as possible. If you want parts of your garden for vegetables and flowers, it is best to cordon these off, because otherwise the chickens will peck at things like tomatoes and eat your flowers. They will most likely lay eggs around the garden, rather than in nesting boxes, so you'll need to be a bit of a detective to find where the eggs are to collect them. If you have many chickens, a lot of space, and know it's free from predators, then free-range chickens can be a good choice. Predators won't attack if they see humans there, but they're not daft and will notice your activity pattern and attack after you have left.

Cages

You can keep chickens in cages in a barn or garage. You can also put them on trees or walls outside. Each hen should have a minimum space of 2 square feet, they need space and room to stand upright. They could either have wire or solid flooring. If you decide to keep chickens in cages, this will prepare them for things like breeding or shows if you show them. If you have a solid flooring, it can be more comfortable for the chickens, but wire floors are easier to clean. Wire floorings can hurt chickens' toes, so I'd advise against this wherever possible. Chickens who are housed in cages often lack exercise, which can cause metabolic disorders. If

you have the cages outdoors, then you need to ensure the hens are protected from adverse weather conditions. Because Bantam chickens are smaller and need less space, these are a popular choice for people who keep chickens in cages. If you have a wire floor, the gaps should not be more than 1.5",

to prevent the chickens from getting their claws stuck and injuring themselves. If you have caged chickens, you can let them get some exercise while you clean out their cage, but do ensure they are safe from predators when you do this.

Shelter and a Run

This is seen as an ideal scenario for those who aren't keen on the fully free-range or cage options. It provides good shelter from adverse weather and allows the hens to safely rest at night, but they also have a safe outdoor space where they can walk around without fear of being attacked by predators. It allows the chickens to experience space, sunshine, and fresh air, all of which are important for happy, healthy chickens. It's ideal if the coop is big enough for you to walk into to clean it out, feed your chickens and give them water, and collect the eggs. If you feel for any reason it's not safe for the chickens to be in the run, you could keep them in the shelter area. Shelters and runs do take up more space in your garden, and if you don't already have a large shed or store house to convert, it can be expensive, but personally I think it's worth it.

Chicken Tractor

A chicken tractor looks like an upside wheelbarrow made from mesh/chicken wire. It is a movable chicken pen, which has 2–4 wheels. They come in various sizes. They can have a roofed area where chickens can lay their eggs. They will have water sources, feeders, and a roost. They don't have any flooring. You can move the chicken tractor to different parts of your garden, where the chickens can graze, safe from predators.

The benefits of this are that the chickens will find insects to eat, which supplements their diet of pellets and grains, giving them much needed calcium. This will help them develop good eggshells. You can move the chicken tractor into the sun on winter days or into the shade on hot summer days. Your garden will be naturally fertilized from chicken manure. You can move the tractor to parts of your garden where you want your chickens to eat garden pests. It is possible to build your own chicken tractor upcycling wooden pallets or fencing.

Having lots of fresh air will help keep your chickens free from disease. They're low maintenance and don't need a lot of cleaning because you can move it from place to place. It does make cleaning quite simple, because in a coop you need to move the chickens whilst you clean the coop, but using a chicken tractor it's easy to move them.

A chicken tractor isn't as sturdy as a more permanent coop. I would worry about this in very windy weather, and it doesn't protect the chickens in adverse weather when there's lots of snow, rain, or really hot sun. It's not as safe as a more permanent coop in terms of protecting your chickens from predators. If it rains, the chickens' food will likely to get wet. You may need to bring a chicken tractor indoors during the winter months.

You may decide to use a chicken tractor in the day, but a coop at night—this option can work well. If you have a chicken tractor, ensure that you rotate its locations. Never put the chicken tractor on uneven ground, because if it isn't flush to the ground, the chickens can get out from under the gaps.

Chicken Shelter Considerations

Chickens need to have shelter, which keeps them out of the harshest elements: the blistering sun, howling wind, rain, or freezing snow. They need to be pleasantly warm and dry.

Size

Chickens need space, and not to be too crowded. If they are too crowded, they will peck one another. Chickens like having space to roam. Also, once you start raising chickens, it can be addictive and you are likely to add more hens to your flock, so starting off with a bigger space allows you to add more, rather than having to extend your housing area. You should have 3–4 square feet per chicken inside the coop, and outside chickens should have 8–10 square feet per chicken in the run area. It's good for chickens to have a variety of levels and ramps to make the coop more interesting and have places to climb and relax. It's not sensible to buy coops that are only the size of a rabbit or dog hutch, these are just not big enough long term for chickens.

Location

If you live in a location where there is a lot of snow, the coop needs to be tall so that if it snows heavily, then you can still get into the coop to clean it. You need to be able to tend to your chickens in any weather, so it does need to be accessible. A shaded location is a good plan so that the coop doesn't overheat in the summer. Chickens will become uncomfortable if it's too hot for them. You could place it under a tree or a tarp for shade. You can have the coop facing the south, with windows on the east and west sides so that your chickens can get some sun.

You need to ensure that the coop has adequate drainage and isn't going to get puddles in the winter due to rain and snow. It's uncomfortable for chickens to get covered in mud, and can lead to parasites and diseases. Chickens do want some sun because the sun's rays will kill bacteria in the coop and dry up ammonia.

Insulation

Coops should be cool in the summer and warm in the winter. You need a good flow of air to keep the place ventilated, but not too drafty so as to cause chills. Be careful not to insulate with Styrofoam because the chickens will peck this and rodents will be attracted to it as well. You could attach insulation to the base of the coop on the outside.

Ventilation

Coops do need proper ventilation all the time, summer and winter. If they don't have it, the coops can become too moist from breathing and pooping (which contains ammonia), then the coop may become damp and this will lead to health issues. Chickens do poop a lot. If your hens appear too hot, then you need to add more ventilation holes. It is good in the summer to ventilate the chicken coop with windows and vents on the roof. Having good ventilation will make your chickens healthier. Hens also want lots of natural light and sunshine through their windows, and it makes it easier for you to clean the coop if you can see what you're doing.

Storage Space

There are regular activities that you'll need to do when you go to the chicken coop, such as feeding the chickens, changing bedding, scooping out poop, and so on. So, it's good if the coop has a storage space for grain, bedding, a scoop, and other tools. You need to be able to keep the chickens' feed dry and safe from rodents too.

Nesting Boxes

You require a nesting box for every four hens you have, but if you have more boxes than this, this is all the better. You may find that the hens pick a preferential nesting box and squabble about who has it. It is important to keep the bedding for your chickens changed regularly, fresh and dry. Chickens who lay eggs want comfort and a private space to lay their eggs. They like their nesting boxes in a secluded area in the coop with low light.

It can be worth putting in full-size nesting boxes (even if you currently have bantams) so that if you want to introduce full-size chickens in the future, you can easily do this.

The roofs of the nesting boxes should be very sloped to prevent the hens from perching there. There should be a 4" lip on the lower part of the nesting box, this will stop eggs from rolling out. You can add curtains over the nesting boxes, which will give your hens more privacy for egg laying.

Nesting boxes should be approximately 15 inches high and wide, and approximately 12 inches deep. Keep the nesting boxes away from the roosting perches so that they are not pooped upon. Some nesting boxes are on the outside of the coop, and have a hinged door on top so that you can easily gather the eggs without the need to go into the coop.

Roost

A roost is a perch, and chickens will congregate on it together to sleep at night. The roost should be higher than the nesting boxes, but its lowest bar shouldn't be more than 18" high so that heavier breeds can still get on it.

There should be space on the roosting bars in order to prevent chickens from pooping on one another. There should be 8 inches of space on a roost per chicken at a minimum. In summer when it's warm chickens will want more space on the roost.

If a chicken is being bullied by another, it should have space to sleep away from the bully. It's best to use wood planks or sticks rather than tree branches for a roost, as branches can cause mites. You don't want the roosts near the chickens' food either in order to prevent them from pooping in the food. Generally, chickens like to be high up and they will try to get the best roost positions higher up.

Flooring

You can have a dirt floor, wooden floor, or concrete. If you have a dirt floor, predators can dig their way in, and rodents too, so you would need to sink fencing into the ground around the coop to prevent this.

If you opt for a wooden floor, it can absorb moisture, and mites can infest the coop. If you put vinyl flooring over it, this will help.

Finally, concrete flooring is best really, it's easy to clean and will prevent predators and mites.

Bedding

There are different bedding materials you can use as litter for your flock in the coop. They all have their pros and cons, which will be discussed below.

Straw is relatively accessible and helps keep chickens warm if you live in a colder climate. It's not very absorbent, however, and needs to be changed frequently. Because it's not absorbent, it tends to stink and can become difficult to clean.

Wood shavings, most commonly pine and cedar, are easily accessible, they're often sold at feed stores. They also have great absorption and because of that they are easy to clean and provide excellent odor control. They can be a bit more pricey than other bedding materials and they can be dusty, which is not great for your chickens' respiratory system.

Sand can be a time-consuming kind of litter to manage, but people who use it swear by it. It's often used with deep litter method (more about that later), and it's simply turned, meaning that when it becomes soiled, you simply turn it to bring the clean sand from the bottom to the top. It clumps just like cat litter and chickens can use it for dust bathing, which they will definitely love. It's also great for odor control. It doesn't compost, however, and you can't use it as a fertilizer. It also can be dusty and provides less cushioning, so your chickens will have a rougher landing when jumping from the roosts.

Some people use recycled paper, but I would recommend leaving it for the brooder box. It takes a lot of paper to cover the entire coop, but it's great for chicks in a brooder box, as it's soft and gentle for the babies. While it absorbs quickly, it needs changing often, so you'll have to clean your coop several times a week, at least twice weekly. And it's not great for odor control.

Deep Litter Method

Before we get to the deep litter method, let's first talk about the non-deep litter method. With the non-deep litter method, you would remove the old bedding weekly with your regular coop cleaning. You can do it bi-weekly or even monthly if you have a smaller flock, although I suggest cleaning your coop and changing the bedding weekly.

With the deep litter method, you would simply add fresh bedding on top of the old one, which in turn will create a compost pile with the chicken poop at the bottom. The benefits of the deep litter method are that it's easier to manage than changing the bedding weekly, you're creating a compost pile right in the coop, and it helps retain warmth, which is good if you live in a colder climate.

I would suggest using pine shavings for the deep litter method. Straw doesn't absorb well, so it's not a great choice for this method. Start with 4–6 inches of pine shavings as bedding. Then, turn the bedding weekly and add some fresh bedding on top. The rate at which the decomposition happens will depend on the climate you live in, how many chickens you have, how often you turn the litter, and how moist it is in the coop. The coop shouldn't smell bad and it shouldn't smell like ammonia. If it smells like manure or ammonia, you need to add more bedding and turn it more frequently.

Once the bedding gets to about a foot, you need to clean it out. Some people clean it to return the litter to 4–6 inches, others remove all the litter to do a thorough cleaning. Leaving some litter will help jump start the next batch. Do not use diatomaceous earth inside the coop if you're using the deep litter method. It's a drying agent and it will dry out the litter and prevent it from composting.

Lighting/Electricity

It's really sensible to have electricity in a chicken coop so that you can use heat lamps to keep your chickens warm in the winter. You can also heat the drinking water in the winter to prevent it from freezing over. It can be useful for you to see what you're doing when you check on the chickens, clean them out, and change their food, water, and bedding.

In the winter, the artificial light can help hens keep laying eggs too. Unless you are an electrician, it is advisable to have the electricity set up by a professional, to prevent any tragedies involving extension cords, rodents chewing through wires, or other malfunctions.

Temperature

Chickens can get too hot in extreme heat conditions. Conversely, they don't like too cold weather either and can suffer from frostbite. They ideally like a temperature of around 72°F.

Waterers and Feeders

You need to have plenty of waterers and feeders that you can easily access, and have them positioned at a height that the chickens won't poop in.

Droppings Board or Hammock

A droppings board or hammock makes collecting the poop much easier.

Dust Baths

Having a dust bath is really important in the coop, it can be a box of sand that they go in when they want, especially in the colder months, if they don't go out in a run, or there is snow and ice on the ground. Having a bath in dust can help prevent parasites. We have used things like an old children's paddling pool or old car tires to create dust baths in the past, and this allows the hens to keep their feathers clean and in good health.

Automatic Doors

You can purchase and install automatic doors, but these generally aren't advisable. It's important to check that all your hens are in and roosting for the night. If they're not, this can be a sign that some of them are ill or injured. Automatic doors could lock a predator or rodent inside, and they can also malfunction.

Should You Buy or Build Your Own Coop?

The decision as to whether you should buy or build your own coop usually depends on how good your DIY skills are. Even if you buy one, it will need assembling. Try not to be swayed by a coop that is pretty, but not practical. It needs to be sturdy, durable, and weather resistant.

Costs of coops vary from a couple of hundred to a couple of thousand dollars. Once you have a pre-made coop, it can be hard to customize it. If you don't own power tools, it can be quite expensive to buy or rent these, though you could ask friends or family if they have any you could borrow.

You can look at plans for chicken coops and ensure that yours has room for the chickens to sleep, lay their eggs, and an open run. You can customize yours accordingly if you are building it yourself. Things that you need to remember to include in a good coop are:

1. Nesting boxes. You will need to put clean bedding in this, and this is where you will gather the eggs from.

2. The coop needs a door you can walk in to be able to put in clean food, water, clean out the poop, and gather the eggs. The floor will protect chickens from predators and add protection against adverse weather conditions.

3. The door should have a latch/padlock to stop raccoons from getting in, if they live in your area. You also don't want any people stealing your chickens!

4. Wire can stop predators, but will also allow air to circulate.

5. You need to ensure the flooring is predator-proof so that rats, mice, and squirrels don't dig under the coop. You will require small mesh fencing buried into the ground around the edge of the coop.

6. If you are building the coop, you can leave space under the enclosed area, for trays that can collect droppings and make cleaning much easier.

If you decide to build the chicken coop, this may cost half of what you would spend on a ready-made coop. This may also depend on whether you already have any material to use, the tools you have, and whether you will upcycle any materials from around your garden. Chicken Coop Kits, whilst they have been designed, do require a lot of assembly.

If you need to save money, have good DIY skills, some knowledge of construction, and have the time to build a coop before your chickens arrive, then building a coop could be a good option for you. If you don't have these skills and time, then it may be better to buy one. If you decide to buy, you needn't always buy brand new, you could purchase a pre-owned coop from someone who no longer needs it.

If you decide to do this, ensure that it is clean, and that there have been no infectious diseases in the coop previously. Even if the previous owner says there haven't been, I would thoroughly disinfect every inch of the coop to ensure it is safe for your beloved chickens prior to use. If you're buying a brand new coop, it is sensible to ensure it has a warranty with it so that you know it will last and be durable and is protected for a period of time.

I would suggest looking for coop plans online if you're looking to build a chicken coop by yourself rather than buy a pre-fabricated one. There are a lot of good and detailed plans that are often free too. However, not all of them are good enough to follow. With that said, I've made a complimentary eBook where I've chosen 10 best-looking, easiest-to-build, or the cheapest chicken coop plans available that you can realistically build in your backyard. You can download the complimentary eBook by clicking here. Just leave your email and we will send you the book right away. Alternatively, please send me an email to maxbarnesbooks@gmail.com and I will send you the book as soon as humanly possible.

Runs and Yards for Chickens

Chickens do need outdoor space, and it's up to you whether you make this contained or free range. If you have free-range chickens, you do need to ensure that they can't be attacked by predators. Chicken wire on its own will not prevent predators. To keep predators out, you also need 0.5-inch hardware cloth to enclose the run and coop windows. It's better to use screws and washers, rather than just staples to fix the cloth; and as previously mentioned, you need hardware cloth on the ground and dug into the ground around the perimeter of the run to stop predators from tunneling their way into your chickens. If you live in an area with bears, you should have an electric fence around your backyard too. If you want to prevent flying predators, cover the run from above with hardware cloth.

Sometimes your living situation may mean that you're not able to have free-range chickens. If this is the case, having a run can be a really good option, to allow your chickens a sense of freedom, fresh air, and room to stretch their legs and wings and exercise without having to sit and watch them all the time, as realistically most people don't always have the time to do that. By having a chicken run, this can prevent predators from getting to them. It can also keep your neighbors happy if chickens have previously strayed onto their property, and it can prevent the chickens from eating your plants.

 Chickens do love the outdoors and rooting in grass and leaves looking for bugs and insects, sunning themselves, and having a dust bath. The more space you can use for your run, the better. If chickens don't have enough space, they may become bored or aggressive. More space will reduce disease. If you only have a small garden, ensure you don't fill it with too many hens. Hens are sociable though and do like company.

With your run, do ensure that you have small gaps, because things like rats and weasels can squeeze through very small holes. Cover the top of the run to prevent birds of prey from attacking. Padlock gates and doors. If you put run-on grass, it is likely that the chickens will soon scratch it up, and make it muddy in winter and very dusty in the summer.

Chicken tractors can be a good way to move chickens around and let them help with the weeding and pest control as they go. You may decide to put pine pellets on the floor of your chicken run, they will soak up mud and moisture and leave the run floor covered in sawdust.

Another option would be wood chippings or mulch. You can also use coarse sand. It's probably best not to use straw as it will retain water, create spores that can contribute to respiratory issues and infestations of mites.

You can ensure chicken runs are sloped or have a paving slab base in order to prevent water from gathering in the run. Ensure that your chickens always have something else to stand on other than just mud, so this could be concrete, slabs, pallets, something where they can dry their feet and be clean. This will help prevent health issues.

If your chicken run doesn't have natural shade from a tree, you can put a tarpaulin across a corner of it in the summer months, to give the run some shade and prevent your chickens from overheating. You could also grow climbing plants up the side of the run if your chickens don't eat them.

You can build your own chicken run just like you can build your own coop. It is important to make it really secure so that your full-grown chickens that have started laying eggs aren't attacked by predators, such as foxes, possums, raccoons, snakes, and hawks. It's much better for chickens to have space to run about and stretch their legs rather than being locked up in their coop. If you want to build your own run, the type of supplies you will need include:

- Wooden posts or half posts or T-posts
- Welded wire fence
- Zip ties
- Poultry net staples
- Metal wire
- Hardware cloth that has ½" or ¼" gaps. It is NOT advisable to use normal chicken wire because this won't keep out predators. Adding this hardware cloth with very small gaps at the bottom of the run will help with predators. If you can build the entire run out of this—great, but if you need to minimize cost, then just putting it at the bottom is best.
- Heavy-duty deer fencing

- Gate

- Tape measure

- T-post driver or post hole digger

- Pliers

- Wire snips

- Hammer

- Tamper

You will need to work out how large you want your run to be based on where the coop is, and if other sections of the garden are already partitioned. If you want your run to protect against hawks, then it's good for it to be about 4 ft wide, because hawks want a wider space than this to land in. Ensure you have a space for a gate and that the coop is against one side of the run.

If you're using wooden posts, you can use a post hole digger to dig 2 ft holes for them. If you choose to use T-posts, you can hammer them in with a T-post driver. When you put your posts in, they should be spaced every six feet apart. You'll need to pack the post hole with dirt and a tamper.

Then, you'll need to attach the fencing. Before attaching it, make sure the fence is on the ground level along the whole path. You can attach the fencing on the ground level, but I highly recommend digging a trench and burying the fence 6–12 in. into the ground to provide additional protection from the predators. Once it's positioned correctly, you can wrap one end around the first post and attach it using zip ties. Then roll out the fencing along the rest of the posts and wrap the other end around the last post, once again securing it with zip ties. Walk along the fence and make sure it's positioned correctly. Once you're happy with the fence position, you can attach the fence to wooden posts using ¾-inch poultry staples or if you're using T-posts, use pieces of wire to attach. It's highly likely your run will be attached to the coop, so depending on how it fits with the run, you can use wire snips to cut an opening for the coop if necessary, and use staples and wire to attach the fence to the coop. You can also attach hardware cloth along the bottom of the fence for additional protection from predators. If you don't want to use hardware cloth, then ensure chickens are placed in the coop at night. If you cover the run with something like heavy-duty C flex 80 round, this will stop overhead predators like hawks. The gate you choose should be wide enough to fit a wheelbarrow through it.

Fencing

I can't stress enough how important it is to ensure the chicken coop is strong and secure and that your grounds are secure too. Predators will try to get to your chickens at night and you certainly don't want that happening. The fencing for your chickens should be at least 5 feet high to prevent your chickens from flying out. If you happen to have a guard dog, it could watch your chickens, or you will need to look out yourself to prevent predators. Hawks and possums will try to prey on your chickens. Most predators will dig at the base of fencing. If you have buried this into the ground, they will just reach more fencing, so this is a good deterrent. You need to ensure that the chicken fencing will last a long time and be a good deterrent to predators.

Some places still recommend chicken wire as fencing for your coop and run. It is reasonably priced, but as mentioned earlier in this section, when looking at runs, hardware cloth can make your runs and fencing much more predator-proof. Hardware cloth is another name for rabbit cage wire, it's usually thicker than chicken wire, and has smaller gaps. If you can afford hardware cloth, this is what I would recommend.

If you have larger predators such as bears, you may need chain-link chicken fencing around your enclosure so that it's harder to get into. Safety fences that are made of flimsy plastic should only be used to contain your chickens very temporarily for a few minutes whilst moving them. You can also get electric fencing, which is inexpensive. Once chickens go into it once, they know not to go near it again and it can really help keep predators out. Aviary netting can protect your chickens from flying predators, such as hawks and owls.

It's a common sense point to make, but one worth mentioning: you should regularly check your chicken fence perimeters for wear and tear. Ensure that no gaps have appeared and look to ensure that no predators have been digging under a part of the fence. It's best to do this regularly and make it a part of your chicken care routine rather than being lax about it and finding out the hard way, once your chickens are attacked.

Our first coop was a repurposed storage shack in the corner of our homestead. It was a good size, and we were able to walk inside it to clean it and collect the eggs easily. It also had a run which was fenced in with a chain-link fence.

Key takeaways from this chapter:

1. Chicken coops need to be weather-resistant, spacious, ventilated, have nesting boxes, roosts, an outdoor area, a dust bath, and be secure to prevent predators.

2. There is a variety of chicken housing options, including free range, cages, shelter and a run, and a chicken tractor.

3. Chickens need 3–4 sq. ft. inside a coop, and 8–10 sq. ft. per chicken in a run area.

4. Ensure that you have stand-up access to a coop. This will make it easier to clean and collect eggs from.

5. A coop should not be too hot or too cold, it should have some sun and ventilation, good drainage, and ideally some storage space.

6. Nesting boxes should be full size, have a 4" lip to prevent eggs rolling out, be 15" high and 12" deep.

7. A roost should have 8" of space per chicken minimum, and they should be positioned away from food and so that chickens don't poop on one another.

8. Floors of coops should ideally be concrete, as these are easier to clean and prevent predators and mites.

9. You should have electricity in the coop—it makes it easier to see what you're doing on dark mornings and nights and it allows you to use heating lamps to keep hens and their water warm in winter to prevent their water from icing over.

10. Have a droppings board—this makes it easier to clean out the chicken poop.

11. Ensure your chickens have access to dust baths.

12. I don't recommend using automatic doors, as they can malfunction or lock in a predator. It's always best to make sure your chickens are in the coop for the night.

13. Put fencing into the ground to provide additional protection from predators.

14. Use hardware cloth instead of chicken wire because it's stronger with smaller gaps.

15. Cover the run from above to provide protection from flying predators, such as hawks and owls.

16. Ensure your run has a gate big enough to get a wheelbarrow in.

The next chapter will look at feed and water for chickens and discuss in detail what chickens eat, the different types of chicken feeds, how to choose feed for your chicken, and water management to make sure your chickens always have access to clean water.

Chapter 4: Feed and Water

This chapter will look at what chickens eat, the types of chicken feed available, choosing a feed to meet the needs of your chickens, and water management. Ensuring that your chickens have good food and plenty of water will mean that you have healthy chickens who should make lots of happy clucking noises each time you bring food to them. If chickens don't have adequate food and water, they may not lay as many eggs, they could suffer from egg deformities, they may pick at each other's feathers and bully other chickens to get the food off them.

You can hang chicken hoppers and water dispensers from the ceiling of a coop and ensure that they reach bird shoulder height. If you have a large hopper, it will hold more feed, and not need topping up as often, but if you take the feed in each night to stop rodents, then smaller feeders are easier to carry.

It is sensible to have space within the chicken coop for a cupboard to store food in so that it is safe, dry, but easily accessible for you to top up the food when required.

What Chickens Eat

When chicks are 0–8 weeks, you can give them 18–20% starter feed crumbles.

When chicks are 8–14 weeks, you can give them 16–18% starter/grower.

Chicks of 15–18 weeks can be given 16% finisher.

18 weeks and upwards chickens can be given 16% layer feed.

When chickens eat greens, like grass or dandelion weeds, they will also need to have a dish of grit to help their digestion so that their crop doesn't become impacted.

It is important to ensure chickens have enough food. If they don't, they will be underweight, and may bully other chickens for their food.

You can share the scraps and leftovers from your kitchen with chickens, and this can give their diet variety. This can be especially good in the winter when grass and bugs have died back. Chickens can eat most meat, insects, fruit, nuts, and vegetables, with some exceptions discussed below.

Food that you should avoid giving chickens includes raw amaranth, apple seeds, avocado (these contain persin which is toxic), never dry uncooked beans (because these contain hemagglutinin and can cause blood clots), remove stones/pits from stone fruits, avoid raw chicken, avoid citrus in case it causes soft eggshells, don't give coffee grounds to chickens, don't give large amounts of cheese to chickens, only give chickens cooked eggs if you do at all, avoid eggplant and eggplant leaves. Don't give them fried, fatty, or salty foods, such as French fries. Don't give chocolate to chickens. Don't give grass cuttings to chickens as they could impact the crop. Don't give maggots to chickens in case it causes botulism. Avoid fat from meat. Beware of wild mushrooms in case they are toxic. Avoid olives cured in salt. If you give chickens too many chives, onions, or garlic, this can cause their eggs to have an unusual flavor. Try to avoid giving chickens too much bread or pasta, because these don't contain anything of nutritional value to them. Avoid potatoes and their peel because these contain solanine. Some people say it's fine to give chickens potato skin and that this is a myth, but I personally don't with mine. I would always err on the side of caution. Don't give rhubarb to chickens because it contains oxalic acid which can be toxic. Only give cooked rice to chickens, never raw. Avoid chickens eating snails because they can carry gapeworm. Avoid chickens eating the leaves off tomato plants, or green tomatoes, because they contain solanine. Don't give chickens anything containing xylitol. Elephant ears (aka Taro) are poisonous to chickens. Chickens can eat fish, but not buttered or battered/fried.

As treats, it can be nice to give your chickens mealworms. These are high in protein and good for chickens when they're molting. It is actually fairly simple to raise your own mealworms, and this would give you a ready supply. Don't use freeze dried mealworms, as sometimes these can be fed things like Styrofoam, which isn't healthy.

We tend to feed our chickens in the morning and in the evening, chickens like small but frequent portions. We place our chicken feed into a trough, which keeps it clean, dry, and off the floor. Chickens don't tend to overeat. When they've had enough, they stop eating. If you leave feed out overnight, this can attract mice and rats. Many people choose to take in food at night.

As an approximate guide (though breeds/sizes/ages of chickens differ), two large handfuls each morning and evening is usually enough to keep 6 chickens happy. It's good to clean up any old scraps so that they don't attract vermin or insects. When you feed your chickens, ensure that the dominant chickens don't get all the food, leaving none for the others. If you notice this pattern, you could opt to feed them separately.

Chicks will create a mess, and scratch their food all over, they'll mix it with bedding and poop in it. So, you can choose feeders that help to eliminate this mess.

Types of Chicken Feeds

There are lots of different types of chicken feeds, and a lot of different jargon to accompany it, such as 'mash', 'grower feed,' 'medicated' and 'unmedicated.' If you're new to looking after chickens, this understandably can be confusing.

Starter Chicken Feed

This is for baby chicks, and it's generally used in the first 6 weeks of a chicken's life. It has high protein content of 20–24% and it helps chicks to grow. It does need phasing out after six weeks, because too much protein after this age can damage chickens' livers.

Grower Chicken Feed

This is what you should use for your chickens when they're between 6 and 20 weeks old. This does still contain protein of about 16–18%, but it has less calcium than in layer feed. This type of chicken feed allows your chickens of this age to grow, but without giving them too many vitamins or minerals that are required for egg production. When your chickens start to lay eggs, this is a sign that you should move them onto layer feed.

Layer Chicken Feed

This will be the diet that your chickens will be fed on for most of their life. It is a nice balanced diet that contains suitable protein, calcium, vitamins, and minerals, which helps create high-quality eggs. It shouldn't be fed to chickens under 20 weeks of age.

Mash

This is loose chicken feed with a crumbly texture. It can be used for baby chickens for easy digestion, but adult chickens can be fed it too. Some people add water to it, to make it into a sort of porridge. The crumbly texture of this feed can mean that some of it gets wasted.

Crumble

This is a coarser version of mash, it's a bit easier to manage than mash.

Pellets

Pellets are the most common type of chicken feed. They maintain their shape, so if a feeder gets knocked over, they won't necessarily go to waste. They're easy to store. Many people with chickens tend to use these.

Shell Grit

Shell grit is important to give calcium that helps chickens produce good, strong, and healthy eggs. Also, chickens will keep some of the shell grit in their gizzard area, which helps break down their food, making it easier to digest. Chickens know themselves how much calcium they require, so never worry about giving them too much calcium. If chickens don't have access to shell grit, they may develop a condition called Sour Crop.

Chicken Scratch

Chicken scratch should be used as a treat for your chickens and will include cracked corn and grains. This food is nice as a treat, especially in winter to keep them warm, but this isn't the healthiest thing to feed them too often.

Choosing Feed for Your Chickens

You can get medicated or unmedicated chicken feed. A medicated feed will contain coccidiostat to prevent them from getting coccidiosis, which is a horrible disease. If you chicks have been vaccinated against this, then don't give them medicated feed.

You can purchase layers pellets for egg-laying hens, and these will give your chickens the correct protein, vitamins, nutrients, and minerals they require for egg production. They typically contain wheat, maize, salt, sunflower seeds, and oats. You can also give them corn or wheat for variety, and fruit and vegetables daily.

You can buy fermented feed, which will give your chickens more vitamins and enzymes. This food helps your chickens to feel full for longer.

You can get feed for broiler chickens (chickens intended for meat) and this feed contains more protein, which will help chickens grow faster.

Water Management

Chickens should have access to clean, fresh water at all times. An adult hen will drink approximately a pint of water a day, taking small sips throughout the day. If they don't have enough water, this can have an impact on the amount of eggs they produce. Some meat birds may need even more water because they have a fast metabolism and grow quickly. As a rule of thumb, you need 1 waterer for every 10 chickens; however, the more you have, the better.

You need to check that the water does not have wood shavings, dirt, or poop in it, and try to keep it as clean as possible. If you decide to add anything like cider vinegar or vitamins, do only add a small amount, and check that all your chickens are still drinking and haven't rejected the water because of this. Ensure there is no algae or rust in the water dish. You do need to

clean the water containers thoroughly at least once a month to prevent bacteria.

With chicks, the water shouldn't be too hot or cold, but just a nice tepid temperature. You may need to dip the beak of each chick into the water to help them find where the water dish is. You can do the same with food too. With chicks you will want to put some pebbles or marbles in the water dish so that they don't fall in and drown. You may also want to add an electrolyte or vitamin supplement to give them a good start in life. With chicks, you may need to change the water several times a day, as they'll get bedding in it frequently. You may opt to use a heated water bowl, which gives your chickens access to clean water and helps prevents the water from freezing in the winter months.

It is possible to get automatic water dispensers that connect to a garden hose. These automatically fill up when they are emptied. Galvanized waterers allow water to fill up. These work best when off the ground or hung from a rafter. But don't put cider vinegar into one of these, as it will make the metal rust. You can buy plastic waterers too, and you can add supplements to these.

Key takeaways from this chapter:

1. There is different chicken feed for chicks (up to 6 weeks), growing chickens (up to 20 weeks), and laying feed for egg-laying chickens, or broiler feed for meat chickens.

2. If chickens are bullying or pulling out feathers, then check that they all have access to enough food each day.

3. Chickens need grit to aid digestion and keep their crop free from infection.

4. Don't give chickens fried, fatty, or salty foods, uncooked beans, potatoes or potato peel, avocadoes, fruit stones or pips, or citrus fruits.

5. Mealworms or scratch can make a nice treat for chickens.

6. You can give chickens medicated or unmedicated feed. Medicated feed will prevent them getting coccidiosis, but don't give them medicated feed if they've been vaccinated.

7. Ensure chickens have at least a pint of fresh water each per day, keep it clean, and ensure it is not frozen. If you want to add a small amount of cider vinegar or vitamin supplement to the water, ensure you have a plastic rather than metal waterer.

The next chapter will look at health care for your chickens, looking at biosecurity and parasites to be aware of that your chickens could catch. It will also look at signs of a healthy chickens and signs of unhealthy ones. Finally, it will cover common chicken health issues, their symptoms, and treatment.

Chapter 5: Health Care

Chickens are messy, so you need to ensure that feeders, waterers, nesting boxes, and brooder area are kept clean. You need to clean the coop weekly. If bedding gets wet, it will need changing. If you can ever smell ammonia, it is way past the time that the bedding needs changing. Because places like the brooder are warm, and there is poop and pee, this is a perfect environment for bacteria to breed, and therefore they must be cleaned and washed regularly to prevent infection and disease. You should clean feeders and waterers regularly and sanitize them every week. You will end up throwing out feed that has poop in. If you ever see spilled feed, clean it up and throw it out. Don't re-use it because you don't know if it was contaminated by rats or wild birds.

You need to wash and sanitize your hands before feeding chickens. Deep clean the coop at least twice a year, where you clean everything out of it, scrub it all with detergent, then use a strong disinfectant, and allow it all to air-dry before allowing the chickens back into it.

This chapter will cover the topics of biosecurity for your chickens, and common parasites to be aware of that chickens could catch. It will cover the signs of a healthy chicken, and things to look out for that could indicate you have an ill chicken. It will also discuss common chicken health issues, their symptoms, and what you can do to prevent them or treat them.

Biosecurity

Biosecurity means the system you have to prevent your chickens from infectious diseases. Having good biosecurity around your chickens will prevent infections, illness, and death, and reduce the need for antibiotics. It will prevent infection between different flocks of chickens. It will ensure that the eggs your chickens produce are safe for your family or for sale. It will ensure you have healthy chickens, and that you don't need to see the vet so often or spend a lot of money on veterinary care.

Diseases can come from yourself, other people, other poultry keepers, clothing, equipment, shoes, and all wildlife. If you have been to another poultry yard, show, livestock auction, fair, or feed store, to prevent any diseases spreading from there to your chickens, it is best to shower and change clothes and shoes before seeing your own chickens. If you know that there is an outbreak of something live Avian Influenza or Newcastle Disease, then it is best to avoid places with other birds if you possibly can. Don't allow visitors to the house to go and see your chickens.

Get any visitors from high-risk areas to wash their hands, change clothing, and wear disposable shoe covers. If you have a sick chicken that has been isolated from the others, again change clothes, wash hands, and wear clean shoes when going to your other chickens.

As mentioned in the introduction to this chapter, keep cleaning and disinfecting feeders and waterers regularly to prevent disease.

It's advisable to try not to attract wild birds to the areas where your chickens are with bird feeders or bird baths because they could be carrying diseases which can spread to your chickens. Migrating birds, such as waterfowl, can spread disease. Diseases can be spread through air, by water, feathers, droppings, or infected eggs. Try to ensure that your coop and run are closed off to prevent other birds from entering. Avoid having a pond near your chicken coop, as waterfowl may be attracted to this.

Try to prevent rodents, mosquitos, or flies near your chickens. Rats and mice are naturally attracted to grain, and they can jump up to three feet. They have good teeth for gnawing through things. They may eat your hens' eggs if they have the chance and can carry diseases such as Salmonella and Leptospirosis. Ensure your feeders are rat-proof. It's good to keep cats and dogs away from your chickens because you don't know if they've been near any infected birds or animals. Keeping the undergrowth around the coop cut back will prevent rodents who like this type of habitat. Clear up any rotting food. Flies need keeping away from the coop, they can be attracted to dirty bedding, which is why you should always keep on top of this and keep it as clean and fresh as possible. Flies can carry over 600 pathogens that could make your chickens ill.

I would suggest keeping different species separately, for example chickens and ducks, because their needs differ, and ducks require water, and can spread things like Avian Flu.

If you get any new chickens, you should quarantine them before introducing them to your flock to ensure they don't have any diseases. A chicken can look healthy, but may still be carrying a disease. When you quarantine chickens, there needs to be a minimum of 12 yards between the quarantine area and your other chickens because some diseases, like Mycoplasma for example, are airborne. Don't share anything between your healthy chickens and the quarantine area: change your clothes, shoes, and wash your hands between them. Three weeks is a minimum time period for quarantine, but ideally, it should be 30–60 days. If you think you need to test the birds during the quarantine period, then do so. You can check that your chickens do not have lice or mites whilst they're in quarantine. Check that they don't appear to have a cough, or sneeze, or make any gurgling noises, check that their eyes aren't red or watery. Check that they have no discharge from their eyes or nose, that they're not depressed or drowsy, and don't appear to stumble. Ensure that they are eating properly and there are no issues with their poop. If the birds appear healthy after their quarantine, then they can be integrated with the rest of your flock.

If you have a chicken that dies under unusual circumstances, then you could request a necropsy (an autopsy for animals) from the vet to try to ascertain why, and that it's nothing contagious that will be passed onto your other chickens.

A good product to sanitize everything in the coop is Oxine, ¼ teaspoon per gallon of water, it is more effective and safer than bleach. You can use bleach in a 1 part bleach to 10 parts water ratio, or there are other sanitizers, such as Lysol and Virkon S.

Commercial chicken farms are potentially at slightly higher risk of disease than small flocks in a backyard area because large-scale poultry farms have many more chickens in close proximity. But, even as a backyard homesteader, you need to maintain strict hygiene rules to ensure your chickens are as healthy as possible.

Signs of Healthy and Unhealthy Chickens

Healthy Chickens

Healthy chickens are active, curious, and alert. They should feel energized and move freely throughout the coop, run, or backyard.

The condition of a chicken's comb and wattle is a very noticeable sign for healthy birds. They must have a bright color, not dark or dull. Only bright ones are the sign of healthy birds. The only exception is when hens molt or stop laying eggs. Then their combs and wattles will fade to pink or a pale red color and will also shrink in size. When they return to laying eggs, the combs and wattles will change again. That's because when a hen begins laying eggs, her comb and wattles get larger as blood flow increases, which causes them to be a darker red color.

Chickens should have shiny feathers with a healthy sheen, and there shouldn't be any bald patches. Once again, when hens are molting, their feathers won't be as shiny and there may be bald patches. But not to worry, they will grow back. If you have a rooster in your flock, hens can also lose some feathers during mating, which is perfectly normal.

Chickens' eyes should be clear and there should be no discharge. There shouldn't be any discharge from the nose either. Chickens should breathe with their mouths closed, except in very hot conditions. If they are breathing with their mouth open, they could be ill.

Their feet and toes should be straight and not too scaly. The feet shouldn't turn outward.

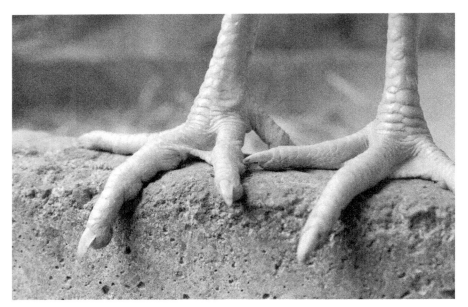

Chickens' vents shouldn't be matted with feces, and there shouldn't be any sores or wounds. Their droppings should be whitish in color and not red or deep green, and of course, chickens shouldn't have diarrhea.

Eggs should have strong shells that are about 0.3 millimeters thick. Strong shells are a sign your birds are healthy and have good nutrition, and that they are receiving the calcium they need.

To keep your chickens healthy, ensure that they have good quality food that is suited to their age and purpose. Give them healthy treats and nothing with too much fat or protein. Keep the chickens free from the stress of predators by protecting their area. Ensure they have a dust bath, things to forage, a secure run, and a safe place to nest and lay eggs. Healthy chickens like to forage for their food. If you have chickens in a run, you could scatter treats such as mealworms, sunflower seeds, or fallen fruit in their bedding to keep them occupied and allow them to forage. If the chickens have long since eaten/scratched all the grass, you could grow sprouted seeds, so they have some greens to peck. You can hang a lettuce at a little height for them to peck at and give them some exercise and activity. There are other things you can purchase for chickens to keep them entertained and active, such as chicken swings, treat balls, or a xylophone. I have previously mentioned dust baths too, which will help to keep their feathers in good condition and free from mites.

Unhealthy Chickens

Chickens hide illness well. If you can detect illness early, you can treat it, and prevent it from spreading to your whole flock. Each time you feed or water the chickens, check them over. Below, you will find the signs of unhealthy chickens and what they could mean. We will take a closer look at common chicken health problems, their signs, and treatments a bit later in this chapter.

If your chickens lack energy and aren't eating, this isn't a good sign. Loss of appetite can happen due to different reasons. It could be something simple, like a heatstroke, or something a bit more serious, like coccidiosis. If your chickens are overweight, they may have Fatty Liver Hemorrhagic Syndrome.

If they aren't laying eggs or they have issues with their eggs, such as soft shells or misshapen shells, this is a sign of ill health. Egg laying can be influenced by a lot of different factors, such as age, molt, weather, stressful environment, and placement of nesting boxes. This will be discussed later in Chapter 8 which is about egg production. Thin, weak shells can be caused by inadequate nutrition or inadequate mineral absorption.

Your chickens' feathers should look glossy and sleek, they shouldn't be dull and there shouldn't be any bald patches. That is, unless they're molting—in which case, patchy feathers are perfectly normal. Otherwise, feather loss around vent and under wings can mean there might be a problem with poultry lice or mice. Feather loss around neck and back usually points to pecking order issues or henpecking. Watch your chickens during feeding time. If they start fighting, pushing, or squawking, then bullying might be the cause of this. Try putting out more than one feed source to discourage henpecking. If you have a rooster in your flock, missing feathers, especially on the back and/or neck, can be from mating. Sometimes a rooster can be a bit rough when mounting hens and missing feathers with no other symptoms may be from this.[12]

If a chicken's head looks swollen, or it has discoloration in its eyes, comb, wattles, or legs, it is a sign of disease and you should inform your vet as soon as you can. Pale, discolored comb is usually a sign of frostbite, and pale and limp comb can be a sign your birds have worms. 13

Chickens' eyes should be clear with no discharge. They shouldn't be cloudy or dull and there shouldn't be any mucus. Swollen eyes with mucus are usually sign your chickens may have cholera. Cloudy and watery eyes could point to conjunctivitis.

14

---

[12] Image from Backyard Chickens: https://www.backyardchickens.com/threads/big-bald-spots-on-both-sides-of-neck-why.305898/

[13] Image from chikchikchicken.com: http://chikchikchicken.com/index.php/2020/06/09/how-to-recognize-a-sick-chicken/

Coughing or sneezing is a late-term symptom, but it's not a death sentence. If you see one of your chickens coughing, act fast to first save your hen, and second, keep any possible contagious illnesses from the rest of your flock. You should separate your sick chicken until you can find out what is making her cough. This will help prevent any illness from spreading throughout your entire flock.

First, look at the condition of your chicken coop. Is there adequate airflow? Are the walls covered in dust? Sometimes a cough is just a reaction to a dirty coop. If there are no other symptoms, clean your coop and see if it helps. Check the bedding in your coop as well. If it's wet or moist, it can cause your chickens to cough from the ammonia smell that is given off from wet bedding. Remove the wet and replace it with a fresh layer to see if this helps. If your chicken has a wet and/or raspy cough which can sometimes be accompanied by a running nose, then there is a good chance your chicken has pneumonia or Chronic Respiratory Disease (CRD). Both of these conditions can be life-threatening and spread throughout your flock. It is important to contact a vet so you can get antibiotics to treat these conditions.

If the chicken staggers or seems unable to stand properly, it can point to bumblefoot, Marek's, or Newcastle Disease. If you noticed your chickens have raised and inflamed scales on their legs, it's most likely scaly leg mites.

If your chickens have diarrhea, take notice. It can point to a range of illnesses from coccidiosis (diarrhea), or pullorum (white fecal matter), all the way to Newcastle Disease (diarrhea).

Common Chicken Health Issues

Air Sac Disease

Early signs include chickens being weak and poor laying. As the disease progresses, they will start coughing, sneezing, having breathing problems and swollen joints. This disease can be fatal. It can be treated by antibiotics from the vet and there is a vaccine against this. Your

---

[14] Image from Backyard Chickens: https://www.backyardchickens.com/threads/cloudy-eye-in-chicken.712237/

chickens can get this from other chickens or birds, especially wild birds, so make sure their environment is well-protected from other birds. It can also be passed from a hen to a chick through the egg. Keep an eye out for the symptoms mentioned above so that you can catch the disease early on and treat it accordingly.

Avian Influenza

This is more commonly known as bird flu. The main signs of this disease are respiratory problems. Chickens will also stop laying and can have diarrhea if they are sick with the bird flu. Their faces can become swollen and their combs and wattles can become discolored and turn blue. Sometimes they may have dark red spots on their legs and combs. Unfortunately, there is no treatment or vaccine for this and the birds will always be carriers if they get this. Chickens sick with bird flu will have to be put down, and you should cremate the carcass so that no other animals can get infected from it. Be cautious around chickens that are sick with the bird flu, as it can make humans sick too.

Botulism

If your chicken has progressing tremors, it's highly likely it may have Botulism. This can happen if their food or water gets contaminated by dead meat. This disease is not too difficult to avoid. You should keep the coop clean and clean up any dead carcasses you may find near their environment.

These tremors can lead to total body paralysis. This is a serious disease. If you catch the disease early on, you can mix 1 teaspoon of Epsom salts with 1 ounce of warm water and give this to your chicken daily by dropper. If the disease has progressed, you'll need an antitoxin which you can buy from your local vet. It can be rather expensive, though.

Bumblefoot

This can happen if your chicken cuts its foot, the cut gets infected, and it begins to swell. It can even swell up the leg. It can be treated by performing surgery, you'll want to contact your vet to get it done. If not treated, bumblefoot can be fatal. Keep an eye on your chickens' feet and clean and disinfect any wounds or cuts to prevent the disease from setting up.[15]

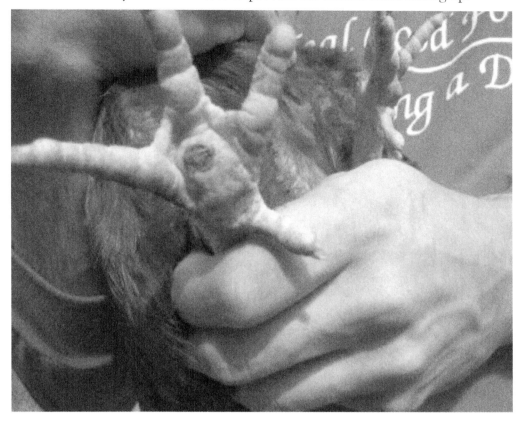

Candidiasis

This is also known as thrush and is caused by a fungal yeast called *Candida albicans*. It is sometimes called 'sour crop' or 'thrush'. It's a disease of the alimentary tract of chickens, and it can affect the mouth, crop, gizzard, or vent of chickens, and will cause thick white patches on their skin.

Signs of candidiasis include dejection, poor appetite, slow growth, and diarrhea. The outward signs of candidiasis aren't very obvious, birds simply look thin and lacking energy. You can prevent candidiasis in your birds by following a good hygiene routine. Dirty feeders and

---

[15] Image from Morning Chores: https://morningchores.com/chicken-diseases/

waterers are perfect places for the yeast to grow, which is why it's important to clean them regularly. Thrush can be related to stress, so ensure nothing is causing your birds to be stressed. You can control the spread of Candida through drinking water with chlorination at 5 ppm, which is about 5 drops of Clorox per gallon of water. Alternatively, you can add a tablespoon of apple cider vinegar to a gallon of water.

There are respiratory antifungal treatments if your bird has a respiratory condition. Generally, treatment includes Nystatin (100 ppm in feed) for 7–10 days, copper sulphate (1 kg/ton feed) for 5 days, or copper sulphate (1gm/2 liters water) for 3 days if approved locally. Keep in mind that long-term antibiotic use encourages yeast infections, so use them only when it's absolutely necessary after consulting with the vet. You will need to deep clean and disinfect your coop if your birds are sick with candidiasis.

Coccidiosis

This is caused by protozoan parasites. If your chickens are looking like they're lacking energy and are weary, if they look pale or have ruffled feathers, these are the signs of coccidiosis. One of the most common signs of coccidiosis is blood or mucus in chickens' droppings. Other signs include a bird huddling as though it's cold, diarrhea, decreased food and water consumption, weight loss, and laying eggs inconsistently or failing to lay eggs completely. As with many other diseases, good hygiene is the key to preventing coccidiosis.

Coccidiosis is treatable if caught early enough. You'll need to treat your whole flock if one of your birds becomes ill. You need to isolate sick hens and clean the coop thoroughly. Amprolium is commonly used to treat coccidiosis. It's a liquid that is administered by adding it to the chickens' water supply and it stops parasites from multiplying. If your chickens are really sick, you might have to administer it orally, as it's highly likely they won't be drinking enough to take in the treatment. Amprolium is available over the counter, but if you have any concerns, you can always contact your vet for professional advice on how to treat your flock.

You can also get medicated feed to give to chickens, which contains coccidiostat that prevents them from getting this. You can also get chickens who have been vaccinated against it.

E.coli

If your chickens have particularly ruffled feathers, this can be a key symptom of E.coli. Other things to look out for include your chicken being restless, depressed, not eating, having a cough or labored breathing.

Once again, good hygiene is the key to preventing and controlling E.coli. Increased dust and ammonia levels and higher litter moisture irritate the respiratory epithelium and provide an opening for E. coli infections. Clean your coop and change the bedding regularly, keep the feeders and waterers clean, and remember to wash your hands regularly.

E.coli can spread to other chickens through chicken poop or contaminated eggs. This is something that can be passed on to humans too, so always keep washing your hands. An antibiotic, often Enrofloxacin, can be given to chickens by a vet to reduce E.coli. Always quarantine any sick birds away from the others.

Fowl Cholera

This is a contagious bacterial disease from the bacterium *Pasteurella multocida,* and it can be deadly. It can cause chickens to become lame and have swollen wattles. If your chickens have ruffled feathers, aren't eating properly, have diarrhea, a cough, eye, nose, or mouth discharge, then you should get them checked for this. This is a disease that can spread through air.

Biosecurity, good rodent control, and good hygiene are essential for preventing fowl cholera. You can give your chickens bacterins at 8 and 12 weeks, as well as live oral vaccine at 6 weeks.

Water soluble antibiotics, such as sulphonamides, tetracyclines, erythromycin, streptomycin, or penicillin, can be given as treatment. The disease often recurs after medication is stopped, necessitating long-term or periodic medication.[16]

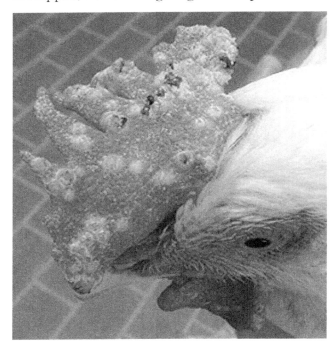

Fowl Pox

If you notice your chickens have white spots on their skin, scabby sores on their combs, white ulcers in their mouth or trachea, and they stop laying—these are all signs of Fowl Pox. You should isolate sick chickens if you notice this, give them soft food and a warm place to recoup. Chickens can get this from other sick chickens or mosquitoes. Fowl Pox is contracted by air. You can get your chickens vaccinated against this.

[17]

Infectious Bronchitis

If you hear your chickens coughing, sneezing, or snoring, and notice secretions from their nose and eyes, they may have Bronchitis. They will stop laying if they have this. This is a viral disease, and it spreads fast by air. To treat Bronchitis, you need to isolate sick chickens, and they need a warm and dry place to recover. You can give them warm herbal tea. There is a vaccine against this.

---

[16] Image from True North Life: https://truenorthlifeblog.com/5-common-chicken-diseases-and-how-to-treat-them/
[17] Image from Morning Chores: https://morningchores.com/chicken-diseases/

Infectious Coryza

The signs of this disease include chickens having swollen head, combs, and their eyes can become swell shut. They will stop laying, there can be moisture under their wings, and there can be discharge from their eyes and noses. Unfortunately, there is no treatment or vaccine for this. If your chickens have Coryza, they will have to be put down. If not, they will remain carriers of the disease and will infect the rest of your flock. Discard the body after you put the sick chicken down by either cremating it or deep burial so that no other animals come in contact with it.

Marek's Disease

This is a disease which can cause inflammation and tumors in the nerves, spinal column, and brain. Birds can become paralyzed in their legs or wings, or may have a head tremor. Birds that have this cease to eat and they can develop sores. If you notice your bird isn't eating, or has lost weight, or looks pale, or their comb is shrunken, these are all typical signs of Marek's disease.

The outcome for birds with Marek's is not good, sadly, with no cure or treatment. Vaccination of day-old baby chicks is the most dependable way to prevent the disease.

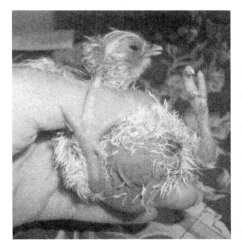

Mushy Chick

This disease affects chicks, and if they catch this, their midsection will be enlarged, inflamed, and blue-tinted. They will look drowsy and weak, and they will have a really unpleasant scent. This disease can spread from chick to chick, so you'll need to separate sick chicks from the rest. Chicks can get this from a dirty surface if they have a weak immune system, which is why it's important to keep their environment clean. It can be sometimes treated with antibiotics from your vet; however, there is no vaccine against the disease. Be cautious when handling sick chicks, as the bacteria that causes the disease can also affect humans.[18]

Mycoplasma

This can cause chickens to have foamy eyes, cause them to sneeze or have nasal discharge, and their eyelids may be swollen. If you have egg-layers, they may not produce as many eggs. This is quite a common disease in backyard chickens. Some birds may die from this. Other chickens will carry the disease, but not display symptoms.

Biosecurity and good hygiene are essential for preventing mycoplasma. Antibiotics may reduce clinical signs and vertical transmission, but do not eliminate the infection. The disease is usually mild, but no treatment can prevent the birds who've had it from becoming carriers for life. Mycoplasma is sensitive to a number of broad-spectrum antibiotics, including tylosin and tetracyclines. I highly recommend contacting your vet for professional advice on how to treat your birds.[19]

Newcastle Disease

Symptoms include breathing problems, discharge from nose, eyes can look murky, and chickens will stop laying. Also, chickens' legs and wings will become paralyzed and their necks twisted. This disease is carried by wild birds. This disease is more dangerous for chicks, as they

---

[18] Image from Morning Chores: https://morningchores.com/chicken-diseases/

[19] Image from British Hen Welfare Trust: https://www.bhwt.org.uk/hen-health/health-problems/mycoplasma/

can die from this, while older birds will recover in most cases, and won't be carriers afterwards. There is a vaccine against this.

Pullorum

This disease can affect both chicks and adult chickens, and it affects them differently. Chicks will become inactive, will have white paste all over their backsides, and have breathing difficulties. Adult chickens will start sneezing and coughing and will stop laying. This is a viral disease. Your chickens can get it from wild birds or contaminated surfaces. Unfortunately, there is no treatment or vaccine for this disease. If your chickens catch this, they will have to be put down. Make sure to discard the carcass by either cremation or deep burial so that no other animals can get infected from the corpse.

Salmonella

Salmonella are bacteria that can cause acute septicemic disease in chickens. Sings include your chickens looking depressed, they may appear weak, and have diarrhea. If they're young and still growing, it may seem like their growth has slowed.

They may be given oxytetracycline, neomycin, and bacterial culture to treat them. You need to manage water so that chickens with this aren't spreading it to other birds. Once infected, birds may always remain carriers for life. Some Salmonella strains are resistant to antibiotics, and prevention is always better than cure.

Biosecurity, good hygiene, and a solid cleaning routine are vital for preventing salmonella. Always wash your hands before and after dealing with your chickens and keep the chicken coop spotlessly clean to prevent this. You can get your chickens vaccinated against this.

Parasites

Mites

They're parasites which live on the outside of chickens and feed off their blood. Mites are tiny, and it's hard to even know if your chickens have got them. The most telling sign is when you examine your chickens, you'll see clumps of mites, especially around the base of the feathers under the wings and around the vent. They look like tiny grey insects, but after they've fed, they turn red. Other signs may include the following: loss of feathers, scabs on legs and feet, pale comb and wattles, reluctance to roost, blood smears on legs, and laying fewer eggs than usual. If there are dirty patches on your birds' feathers, this may be where mites have left droppings.

Mites can often be found around perches at night. Take a torch and a white piece of paper and go to your coop at night. Rub the paper along the bottom of the perches. If it has red smears, it's a telling sign you have mites to deal with.

To deal with mites, you need to take everything out of the coop, including your chickens, of course. Mites are good at finding places to hide, so you need to meticulously clean every inch of your coop. Burn the old bedding and replace it with fresh bedding that hasn't been stored in the coop.

Having dust baths in the coop will allow your chickens to keep themselves clean and free from things such as mites. Other things that may help is using garlic because mites don't like this. You can add this to your chickens' diet, but it may affect the taste of the eggs too. You can add herbs to the coop or spray tea tree or lavender essential oil around the coop. Always ensure to keep the coop clean.

Worms

Chickens can get various types of intestinal worms, and this can easily pass to other chickens through chicken poop. Apple cider vinegar in chickens' drinking water can help prevent this, you can also use garlic crushed in the drinking water too. Chickens can get hair worms which can damage their organs. The most common type, though, is roundworms, and these can be contracted by chickens eating earthworms, and from other wild birds. You can worm your chickens twice a year with a licensed product that you add to your hens' feed, or alternatively, you can buy medicated feed that covers this.

Flystrike

This can happen when a chicken has soiled feathers, and a fly lands on the chicken, and lays its eggs. Then the eggs hatch, and small maggots bury into the chicken's skin. This is a horrific thing for your chickens to experience, as the maggots will start to eat the chicken's organs and eventually kill it. It causes deep painful sores that can become infected. The vent area of a chicken is a common place for this, and it's more common in warm weather.

One of the best things to prevent flystrike is dust bathing, so always give your chickens the opportunity to do this. Also, try to keep the fly population down near chickens. Keep chickens healthy with good food, clean water, and a clean coop and run.

If you see any areas on your chicken that are dirty and contaminated, then these should be cleaned and trimmed. If you have a chicken with flystrike, it needs quarantining away from the other chickens until it has healed. Put vitamins and electrolytes in the drinking water to help the chicken keep hydrated. Bathe the affected area to assess the wound and get rid of as many maggots as possible, remove any you can see. Flush the wound, you can use a syringe to help with this. Dry the area and use a hairdryer on low heat to gently dry it. Use some wound and infection treatment, such as Vetericyn, this is a spray and much preferable to an ointment. Keep doing this a few times a day until the maggots are gone, and the wound has healed. You can also get a vet to treat your chicken too, and they can advise if antibiotics will help, or whether the chicken needs to be euthanized.

Pecking Order

'Pecking order' is a term used to describe the social hierarchy of chickens. Chickens are social animals and like to be a part of a flock. The pecking order is established early on. Chickens can establish it within a few days of meeting each other. Young chicks can bump chests and have stare downs once they are about 6 weeks old. Through these small skirmishes, they establish the pecking order. Chickens who were born and grew up together tend to live in relative harmony as the pecking order is established early on.

It's a flexible structure and it has 3 different layers: rooster to rooster, hens to hens, and roosters to hens.

Pecking order rank determines who gets the best food, water, roosts, nesting boxes, and access to dust bathing areas. A rooster will always be at the top of the hierarchy. If you have more than one rooster, the ones that are lower in rank will crow less frequently and will rarely mate. However, a lower rank rooster can challenge the dominant rooster and take his spot. In the hens' hierarchy, older and stronger birds will be at the top; however, pullets coming to the point of lay will quickly climb the hierarchy ladder. If a bird tries to go out of turn, higher rank birds will peck at her in order to remind her about her place.

While the pecking order provides a sense of order and harmony within a flock, it can also create absolute chaos if things get out of hand. The worst thing that can happen is the pecking order assault. Higher rank birds are relentless, and will injure or even kill lower rank birds who go out of turn.

One way to prevent pecking order issues is to choose and mix your breeds wisely. Docile breeds, such as Orpingtons, Polish, Cochins, and Silkies, can be safely kept together. More aggressive breeds, such as Rhode Island Reds, New Hampshires, and Australorps, should not be mixed with more docile breeds. They will peck at them, and there isn't much you can do to stop it apart from separating them.

There are certain things that can change the pecking order. Adding new birds is the most common reason for a change. Obviously, the existing birds in your flock will try to establish the pecking order, and things can get out of hand sometimes. I recommend adding new birds to your flock at night when everyone's relaxed and wanting to sleep. Also, don't add less than two birds at a time. You can try adding a separation pen if your birds are mean to the newcomers. It's an enclosed area where your new birds can be safe from getting bullied by the older birds. The older birds can pace around the enclosure and look, but they won't be able to get in. When you open the enclosure, make sure to have a safe space where your new birds can run to and hide if things get ugly. We never had any serious integration problems, but it's nice to have some precautions so that your new birds are safe.

As mentioned previously, chicken hide illness well, and that's because other birds will peck at them and try to drive them from the flock or even kill them if they find out they're sick. It may sound awful, but it's a survival tactic. A flock in the wild is only as strong as its weakest member. That's why it's important to isolate sick chickens: not only to prevent them from spreading diseases, but also to keep them safe from being pecked at by other birds. Also, if one of your chickens is constantly being pecked at for whatever reason, you can separate it and keep it in a separation pen mentioned previously for a while. Then you can try reintegrating it as if it was a new chicken to the flock.

Sometimes you may have bully birds in your flock who will peck at everyone. They are usually in the middle of the pecking order and rarely at the top. They can bully other chickens for their food and guard food troughs as if they were theirs and theirs only. If you have a bully in your flock, you can put them in a separation pen for a few days, and then reintegrate them. Sometimes you can even get a few bullies that will form a sort of "bully club". You should separate them from the flock, and then reintegrate them on separate days. This should help break the habit of bullying.

Adding roosters to your flock can be a bit more complicated. If you already have a rooster in your flock and try to add a new one, it will most likely end up in bloodshed. The dominant rooster will immediately try to put the new one in his place. The new rooster, in his turn, can be keen to take over as the main rooster, and will gladly take up the challenge. They will often fight to the death. Sometimes, the only way to keep a few roosters is to make separate flocks so that they each have their own flock and don't compete for the top spot. If you raise roosters together since they were chicks, then this is a different story. They will establish their pecking order in a more friendly manner and will happily coexist in most cases.

Most of the pecking orders issues happen due to the lack of space, food, and water. If you have pecking order issues, make sure your chickens have enough space. Each chicken needs 4 sq. ft. of space in the coop. Chickens should have enough roosting space, at least 8" per chicken, but the more, the better. Ensure your hens have enough nesting boxes, one nesting box for every 4 hens should be enough. You can also try adding additional feeding and watering stations, as higher rank chickens will sometimes guard them and won't let lower rank chickens eat and drink.

Key takeaways from this chapter:

1. Keep coops, runs, feeders, and waterers clean and sanitized.

2. Wash your hands before and after tending to chickens.

3. Deep clean the coop and everything in it at least twice a year.

4. Avoid contact between your chickens and other poultry. Change clothes, shoes (or use disposable shoe covers), and shower if you've seen other poultry, before seeing your chickens. Discourage visitors.

5. Isolate sick chickens.

6. Avoid encouraging wild birds near your chickens as they could spread disease.

7. Prevent rodents and pests, such as flies and mosquitos.

8. Quarantine new chickens for 30–60 days.

9. There are various diseases chickens could catch, and parasites too.

10. Always be on the alert for ill chickens. Look for them being pale, swollen, coughing, sneezing, staggering, ruffled feathers, diarrhea, check chickens' vent area to see there is no poop, which flies could land on. Check that your chickens do not have any sores.

The next chapter will cover routine management of your coop, including daily, weekly, and monthly activities. It will also look at activities that don't occur each month, but should occur a few times a year, such as deep cleaning the coop and preparing the coop and hens for winter.

Chapter 6: Routine management

You will get into a routine for looking after your chickens naturally, but this chapter may be especially helpful to beginners who are finding their feet and worrying about what they should be doing each day and week to best care for their chickens. With time, you will make your own routine that fits in with your lifestyle, but if you're confused and wondering where to start, this chapter breaks down typical activities that occur when you raise chickens.

Often in the mornings, you will let your chickens out of their coop, check their feed and water, and assess their health. In the evening of a day, you will want to lock the hens safely inside the chicken coop. At some point during the day, you should collect the eggs for the day. This here is the very minimum that needs to be done. You will also need to clean out the chicken manure, look after nesting boxes, and more.

This chapter is broken down into daily activities, weekly activities, monthly activities, and activities that occur a few times a year, or specifically in wintertime to prepare the coop and hens for the winter months. The daily activities will look at feeding chickens, giving them clean water, and collecting eggs. Weekly activities include cleaning the coop and dealing with chicken droppings, as well as a health check of the chickens. Monthly activities are managing their bedding, cleaning nesting boxes, and doing a good sanitization of the waterers. Activities that can occur a few times a year include deep cleaning of the coop, and then preparing chickens for winter, ensuring the coop is well insulated to protect from drafts and adverse weather, ensuring that water bowls are heated so that they don't freeze over, and using heating lamps to warm the chickens.

Daily Activities

Release the Chickens

Let your chickens out of the coop into the run at ideally the same time each day. They will look forward to this and enjoy the routine. Chickens love the opportunity to forage in the fresh air and explore. It is best for this to be at sunrise, but if you need to leave before then, you

could open the coop door, and the chickens will make their own way out when it's light, provided your run is safe and predator-proof, of course. It doesn't take a lot of time at all to let the chickens out. The chickens will feel (excuse the pun) cooped up and frustrated if it's light and they can't get out.

Water

Every day, ideally a few times if possible, you need to check the chickens' water, and clean and refill this. If possible, try to have a plentiful supply of fresh waterers so that if one has shavings, straw, or poop in it, they have an alternative one they can drink from. Chickens, just like us, don't want to drink dirty water. It is easy for things to get into the water and mess it up throughout the day. You can use chlorine or oxygen bleach to sanitize the waterers, but do make sure they are thoroughly rinsed after. Again, like us humans, chickens will drink more when it is hot, so it's nice to have plenty of cool water on hand during the hot summer months.

Food

Each day, you will need to feed your chickens. You may decide to use a hanging feeder or feed them a set amount each day. Chickens aren't greedy and won't overeat, they will only eat what they require. Check that any remaining pellet food is dry and not damp. Give fresh food

like corn and greens to them, and ensure any old food is cleared away. The chickens will be hungry when they wake up, so this fresh food should be given to them then.

Collect Eggs

If you have egg-laying hens, you will need to collect their eggs daily so that they are clean and fresh. It shouldn't take long to collect eggs, this isn't a time-consuming task, but very worthwhile. Hens often tend to lay eggs in the morning, after they have eaten. If you're able to collect eggs late morning, this is an ideal time, but naturally this may depend on other life commitments, and you'll need to work out when it fits in with your day.

Check Health

It's important each day to check the health of your chickens and ensure that there are no issues (see previous chapter for the things to look out for).

Check for Cleanliness and Tidy Up

Check the coop is not dirty and remove droppings and old food. Change bedding if required, for example, if it's wet. If you can smell ammonia, the coop needs cleaning as soon as possible.

Ensure Chickens Are in the Coop at Night

Ensure that you have counted all your chickens into the coop at night, to make sure they're all there, and none are ill or injured. Your chickens will most likely head into the coop on their own accord at dusk, and they'll settle on the roosting bars. When you're sure they're all in and safe, you can lock the door of the coop. As previously mentioned, I wouldn't personally advise an automatic coop door, as I think this leads to more issues and problems than benefits.

Weekly Activities

Cleaning the Chicken Coop

A chicken coop should be cleaned at least once a week. You will need to move the chickens to a different place, such as a safe enclosed run, or place them in cages, whilst you clean the coop. If you don't clean the coop regularly, things like bacteria and fungi can grow and this is an environment that mites will thrive in. This will cause issues with your chickens and can be damaging to human health to breathe in too.

When you are cleaning the coop, you will need buckets, a wheelbarrow, bedding, rubber gloves, a face mask, a high-powered spray nozzle, and a compost pile. You will use the bucket and wheelbarrow to move the used bedding and chicken manure.

First, you will need to remove every removable thing from your coop, including feeders, waterers, perches, and nesting box trays. Remove the used bedding and scrape out all the chicken feces, cobwebs, dust, and dirt. Chicken poop will attract flies, rodents, and it will smell really unpleasant. Aim to keep the coop as clean as when you purchased or built it. Scoop out the used bedding and place it in a compost pile. After you're done with the bedding and scraping out all the dirt, grab a hose and spray the inside of your coop down to remove all dust and debris left over from scraping and shoveling. If you use the deep litter method, you don't need to remove the bedding, but turn it instead and add a fresh layer of bedding on top. Needless to say, don't spray the inside of your coop down if you use deep litter method, you don't want to get the bedding all wet.

Next, you will need to disinfect the nesting boxes and the coop. You can use a 1 part bleach to 10 parts water solution, but I would suggest using a natural cleaning agent like vinegar to disinfect the chicken nesting boxes and coop because bleach can be toxic to your chickens. A good product to sanitize everything in the coop is Oxine, you only need ¼ teaspoon per gallon of water, and it is more effective and safer than bleach. If you decide to use vinegar, mix equal parts of vinegar and water and use this cleaning solution to clean your chickens' feeders and waterers, then put them under the sun to dry completely. Let the coop and nesting boxes air-dry. This will help remove the vinegar smell, and the sunlight will help with the disinfection process.

Once everything has dried, put some fresh bedding on the floor and move everything back into the coop. Now you can move your chickens back into their home.

Chickens should have a dust bath available in the coop that they can roll around in, then shake themselves off, and this will prevent parasites. If a chicken has another bird's poop on its feathers, or is ill, you may then decide to bathe the chicken and you will need to do this very gently.

You will also need to clean chicken runs too, so as to prevent things like bird flu from unhygienic environments. Keep the runs free of droppings, and if needed, use a power washer and disinfectant, or a ground sanitizer.

Monthly Activities

Bedding

You will need to change the bedding in the coop at least once a month. You can clean the bedding out once a week or once a month. It depends on the depth of the bedding layer and what litter method you are using. The deeper the bedding layer, the less often you'll have to clean it out.

If you're not using the deep litter method, you'll need to change the bedding during your weekly coop cleaning, or perhaps a bit less often if you have a smaller flock. You can do it bi-weekly or even monthly, replace the bedding when it becomes dirty and/or wet. If you can smell ammonia, you have to clean the coop and change the bedding as soon as you can. I would still recommend changing the bedding weekly if you can, unless you're using the deep litter method.

With the deep litter method, you have to turn the litter and add some fresh bedding every week, and then remove it and deep clean the coop twice a year or when it reaches a foot in height.

Nesting Boxes

You would generally clean the nesting boxes during your weekly coop cleaning; however, if you have a smaller flock, you might have to clean them a bit less often. You will need to remove the old bedding and any broken eggs, clean the nesting boxes thoroughly, and put in fresh bedding. This will give a nicer environment to your hens who lay eggs in the nest boxes, and egg cleaning should be easier.

Sanitize Waterers

While you would normally clean the waterers during your weekly coop cleaning, they should be given a deep clean monthly. You can use 1 part bleach to 10 parts water solution or 1 part water to 1 part vinegar solution. Scrub them with dish soap and warm water, and rinse thoroughly before you refill them for your chickens.

Semi-Yearly Activities

Deep Clean and Disinfect the Coop and Run

A couple of times a year, take absolutely everything out of the coop, and wash the entire thing down using 1 part bleach to 10 parts water solution. Deep clean isn't that much different from your regular weekly coop cleaning. You just have to scrub every inch if your coop down. Just follow your regular cleaning routine and make sure to get into every nook and cranny and clean everything thoroughly.

Pay attention to the roosting bars, they can get really nasty. It may sound strange, but a garden hoe works wonders when cleaning roosting bars. It makes it really easy to scrape all the nasty stuff off without getting yourself dirty in the process. Then, you can use a sponge soaked in vinegar to clean and sanitize the bars.

You can put diatomaceous earth in a coop to prevent mites. The good thing about it is that it's completely natural. Sprinkle it in the nesting boxes and on the coop floor. This way, when your chickens dust themselves, they will be putting diatomaceous earth all over them, which in turn will help deter pests from climbing on them. Don't use it if you're using the deep litter method, as it will dry out the litter and prevent it from composting.

If you ever have any illness in your coop, you should do a deep clean to prevent germs.

Prepare for the Colder Months

You may need to purchase heaters for the waterers, to prevent your chickens' water from freezing over. It is important that they have access to clean water at all times. If you want your hens to keep laying throughout the winter, some people use a light indoor, to imitate daylight. All your hens need roosting space, and this is how they'll keep warm next to one another.

It is good to get into a daily, weekly, monthly, and yearly routine with your hens. By doing this, it will become second nature taking good care of them, and it will keep your hens happy, healthy, and they'll reward you with lovely, delicious eggs. Chickens themselves are quite routine-oriented and will like being let out at a very similar time each morning, and will expect your visits with food, and will like to return to the coop at night.

Key takeaways from this chapter:

1. Stick to a daily, weekly, monthly, and semi-yearly routine. This will help keep things running smoothly and efficiently for you, and your hens will learn to expect it. Plus, the routine will help ensure their health.

2. Daily, release the hens from the coop, change their water, feed them, collect eggs, check their health, clean any poop or old food, and return the chickens to the coop and lock it every night.

3. Weekly, clean the chicken coop.

4. Monthly, change the bedding, sort out their nesting boxes, and sanitize the waterers.

5. At least twice a year deep clean and disinfect the coop and run.

6. Prepare for colder weather, by ensuring there are heaters for the water, to prevent them from icing over.

Looking after our chickens is just all part of our lifestyle. We love and enjoy it. It gets us out of the house more looking after them, and I think it's wonderful to get to know your chickens. Our chickens are a part of our family, and they entertain us. It's easy for us to know if a chicken isn't their normal selves because we know how they typically behave. I enjoy deep cleaning the chicken coop, in the same way that it's satisfying to tidy up your house, wash your car, or put fresh clean sheets on a bed. We still enjoy collecting our eggs in a basket, and it's wonderful to see the different colors of them. The eggs enable us to have so many delicious meals and to do lovely baking. For us, caring for chickens is no more difficult than any other pet, ensuring that they have clean water, are fed properly, and have their needs met, with clean, hygienic accommodation.

The next chapter will look at breeding chickens, from mating your chickens, to incubating eggs, and raising chicks.

Chapter 7: Breeding Chickens

This chapter will cover everything you need to know about breeding chickens. It will look at mating your chickens, incubating eggs, hatching chicks, and raising chicks. Having little fluffy bundles wandering about your garden is an incredible experience, it's lovely to see them grow and develop their own personalities. It's a thrilling experience for both young family members and adults to watch chicks breaking out of their eggs and taking their first steps.

Mating Your Chickens

There are numerous reasons why you may wish to breed chickens. These could include to produce more egg-laying chickens, to produce chickens for meat, to show chickens at competition level, or simply for fun. Breeding chickens will give you a ready supply of chickens who are able to lay eggs in the future, or chickens to produce meat. You need to decide on your purpose for breeding. Then, you'll need to consider if you're going to incubate eggs using an incubator or whether you will let your hens do this naturally. Typically, most backyards tend to have just one rooster. If you want to have a specific pedigree, then you will need to mate a cock to a specific hen to gain the characteristics you want. If you're breeding chickens for fun, then a cock and hen are the key things you require, as the hen will look after her chicks once they have hatched.

January to mid-February is a good time to set up your flock for breeding. If you already have a cock in your flock, or have purchased one specifically, it can be a good idea to create a specific breeding area with their own coop and run, for the cock and approximately 6–10 hens.

The hens for breeding should be at least one-year-old. By mid-February they should start laying. Check to see which ones are laying. Identifying laying hens will be covered in more detail in the next chapter, but here are some things you can do to identify laying hens.

You can pick up your hens gently and look at their vents. A laying hen should have a clean, pink, and moist vent. If it's small, pale, and dry, the hen is not laying.

Laying hens will have worn feathers, especially if you have a rooster in your flock. Their feathers may be broken or rumpled. That's because the calcium in her body is diverted to producing eggs, rather than feather making.

Often the combs and wattles on laying hens will be red. If they are dull and shrunken, it's highly likely the hen is not laying. For hens with yellow pigment, this will strengthen and lessen according to how much they are laying.

You can also resort to trap nesting, although I don't recommend it as it can stress out your chickens. Trap nest is a device that's fitted to a nesting box that traps the hen inside. Once a hen is trapped, simply wait for a while and see if the hen is laying. Don't leave the hen for too long though, as she can become dehydrated, bored, and stressed out, and can even start eating her own eggs, which is a nasty habit that can be hard to break.

You need to identify laying chickens to eliminate the ones that are not laying, as they are not likely to be great layers if you're breeding chickens for egg production. If you want to make a more commercial offering, i.e., selling eggs, then breeding chickens will mean that you won't need to buy new pullets every 3–4 years.

If you have good egg-laying chickens in your flock, ensure that these are first to breed, as genetically they are likely to pass on this good egg-laying trait to any chicks they have. Weight and growth rate are traits that are more important for meat chickens. After you've considered production-related traits, select hens that are the closest to the breed standards, free from defects, vigorous, have docile temperament. Selecting roosters is similar. First of all, the rooster must not be related to any of the hens. Then consider its weight and growth rate. And finally, choose the one that is the closest to the breed standards, and is the most vigorous. You can put leg bands of a particular color on the chickens you've selected for breeding.

Once you've selected your breeders, it's time to move them into the breeding pen. If you've had your hens with a different rooster previously, you'll need to wait for 3–4 weeks to make sure that eggs are fertilized by the new rooster, not the previous one.

If you want a hen's eggs to be fertilized, you may want to ensure that they have a higher protein layer feed and include some oyster shell too. Higher protein means higher fertility and more likelihood of the eggs successfully hatching.

When hens are broody and sit on eggs waiting for them to hatch, it's good to give them starter chicken feed because when they eat, they won't eat for long, as they don't want to leave their eggs, and when the chicks hatch, you'll need this starter chicken feed anyway. If a hen that is sat on eggs doesn't appear to be eating and drinking much, you can gently lift her off the nest and place her next to the feeder.

There are vitamins that you can give to chickens when they are breeding and when they're waiting for eggs to hatch. Vitamin A can be added to their food with broccoli and kale. Vitamin D can be gained via sunlight, and cod-liver oil, and by adding oyster shell as a snack to their food.

Incubating Eggs and Hatching Chicks

You can either decide to use an incubator to hatch eggs or let your chickens do the job for you. You will still have to collect the eggs regularly, even if you plan on having one of your broody hens hatch the eggs.

Collecting eggs and incubating them can be tricky. Ensure your hands are clean when collecting eggs because the eggshells are very porous. It can be good to store fertilized eggs for 24 hours, and up to 7 days, prior to incubation. Store them the pointy end down in an egg box, at 55°F (13°C) in a place that is very humid. You will need to turn the eggs too, to prevent the inner membrane from sticking to the shell. You can tilt the eggs, by storing them with one end of the egg-box raised by something like a book, and in the evening tilt it the other way.

Incubating Eggs with the Help of a Broody Hen

If you let the eggs incubate naturally, this will be done from your hens sitting on them, and they'll only leave the eggs to quickly eat and drink, usually once a day. You should put your broody hen in her own brooder box. You could use something like a rabbit hutch as a brooder box, as she'll have a dark peaceful area to sit on the eggs, and a separate area with food and water. The brooder box will need to be humid. You can cut some turf to fit the brooder box area. Add some turf into the brooder box and make a slight hollow in it to make sure the eggs stay put. Then cover it with fresh bedding. To make sure your hen is broody, you can move her into this brooder box and place some artificial eggs. Wait a day and see if she incubates the fake eggs. She should sit on them all day long and only leave to eat and drink once a day.

Once you make sure the hen is broody, you should introduce your fertilized eggs at night. Typically, a regular-sized hen can sit on 12 eggs, whereas smaller bantam hens usually only manage to cover about 6 eggs at a time. Make sure that your hen covers all of the eggs without having to stretch. It will usually take 21 days for the eggs to hatch. This time will vary from breed to breed.

Your broody hen should take it from there and manage the whole process by herself from start to finish. She will aid the hatching process and will give up on any eggs that aren't going to hatch. Once chicks have hatched, you should remove any remaining eggs and dispose of them. As previously mentioned, some eggs won't hatch, and some chicks will die after hatching. It is very sad, but this is just what happens.

Once the chicks hatch, you'll need to keep the hen and chicks separate from the flock until the chicks are at least 6 weeks old. Most flocks get along just fine, but some chickens can kill young chicks if they get in their way, so keep the newborn chicks and the hen away from the flock in the beginning just to be safe. As mentioned previously, feed your hen and chicks with starter feed. The mother hen will look after the chicks and teach them everything they need to know. Once they're old enough, you can start to introduce them to the flock. It's better to do this at night, when everyone's relaxed and asleep. Their mother will protect them, but keep an eye on the flock, and if you notice that the young chicks are getting bullied, you can separate them again and wait until they grow up some more before introducing them again.

Incubating Eggs Using an Incubator

If you want to hatch quite a number of chicks, then you may decide to artificially incubate them using an incubator. When you artificially incubate, you can see the eggs all the time, but you still need to leave them alone mostly.

Prepare your incubator by washing it thoroughly with a 10% bleach solution and then warm soapy water and rinse it thoroughly. Once it has dried, turn it on and check if it can maintain a constant temperature and humidity. You should place the incubator in an area where temperature is relatively stable and has no drafts.

A forced-air incubator should be set to 99.5°F. A still-air incubator should be set to 102°F. Generally, temperature should be between 99°F and 102°F, ideally 100.5°F. You can keep on top of humidity in the incubator by adjusting the vents on it, but the humidity should be 50–55% during days 1–17, and later increased to 70% on day 18. To check the humidity, you can buy a hygrometer. Only open the incubator when it's absolutely necessary, as the heat will escape, which in turn can affect the incubation process and success of the hatching.

When you are incubating eggs, do remember that not every egg will hatch, so don't expect this, and don't be too disappointed when this happens. Eggs will typically take 21 days to hatch.

Once you've made sure the incubator can maintain the temperature and humidity, you can place the eggs inside of it. This process is known as 'setting the eggs'. I would suggest setting at least 6 eggs at a time. Setting fewer eggs often results in one or no hatchings. Place the eggs in the egg tray of the incubator, with the larger end facing up and the narrow end facing down in the incubator. Set the temperature to 100.5°F with 50–55% humidity.

The incubation process has begun, and next you will have to turn the eggs from day 1 to day 18. Eggs need to be turned to avoid developing chicks from sticking to the shell. Eggs need to be turned at least 3 times a day, and 5 times is even better. Always wash your hands or wear gloves when turning eggs. If you turn the eggs manually, make a mark with a pencil (don't use a pen) to keep track of which eggs have been turned. If you have an automatic incubator, it will turn the eggs for you. Check the user's manual to determine what sort of incubator you have and whether you need to turn the eggs manually.

During days 7–10, you'll need to candle the eggs to determine if the embryos are developing properly. Candling is simply shining a bright light through an egg. It's called candling because they used candles in the past. You can use a flashlight to do it.

A couple of things to remember: don't keep the eggs out of the incubator for more than 5-10 minutes, and don't candle all the eggs at once. Plan to candle a few at a time and leave the rest in the incubator.

Hold the egg with your thumb and first two fingers. Place the flashlight facing the larger end of the egg. You can examine the contents of the egg by tilting the larger end of it slightly.

What you're looking for is a dark spot with spider-like veins. If the inside of the egg is clear and free from dark areas or visible structures, the egg is infertile. If you can see a ring of red, it means there was an embryo inside, but it has died. You can remove this egg. If you can see a dark spot and blood vessels that resemble a bull's eye, there is a live embryo inside. Blood vessels can be seen within 7–10 days of the egg's incubation. By day 18, the embryo should take up most of the egg and look like a dark area within the egg. After candling, return the eggs to the incubator as soon as possible. If you notice any broken or leaking eggs—remove them, as they will likely contaminate the incubator. Candling is mainly used when incubating eggs in an incubator, but there's no reason why you can't candle eggs when a broody hen leaves to eat and drink. You can identify non-fertile eggs and eggs with dead embryos and remove them because they can burst and contaminate the other eggs.

By day 18, the embryo should have developed into a chick and the chick will start preparing to hatch. Here's what you should do to prepare chicks for hatching: stop turning the eggs at day 18 with the larger end of the egg facing up because at this point the chick will position itself for hatching; and increase the humidity to 70% while maintaining the same temperature, which should ideally be 100.5°F.

Chicks will usually hatch around day 21. If the fertilized eggs were cooled before hatching, it may take a little longer. If no chicks hatch at day 21, give them a few more days. When chicks start hatching, do not help them and let them hatch on their own. Chicks typically hatch in 5–7 hours, but it can take up to 24 hours. When all the chicks have hatched, you can lower the temperature to 95°F. When chicks have dried, you can move them into the brooder.

A brooder box can be made quite easily. All you need is some kind of enclosure, like a box, a heat lamp, and some food and water. Each chick needs at least 1 sq. ft. of space. I recommend using pine shavings as bedding on the floor. You can use newspapers, they make really soft bedding which is great for chicks. Straw is fine too. Don't use cedar shavings or any aromatic wood shavings, as they can be toxic to chicks. Make sure chicks get plenty of fresh air, but there shouldn't be any drafts. At first, you'll need to keep the temperature quite high. Keep it between 93°F and 95°F for the first week, and then you can lower the temperature by 3°F–5°F each week for the next 6 weeks. After this, you can introduce them to your flock. If they get bullied, you can separate them again and move them in later, when they have grown a bit more.

It is essential to clean your incubator thoroughly after each hatching so that bacteria and diseases don't spread. Don't use chemical cleaners because this could affect future hatching eggs. Clean it thoroughly with a 10% bleach solution and then warm soapy water, then rinse it thoroughly, just like you did before setting the eggs.

What to Do with Roosters?

When you hatch your eggs, it's inevitable some of the chicks will be roosters. And pretty soon you will find yourself having more roosters than you need or can keep.

Even when you purchase chicks that have been sexed, you can still get a rooster, as sexing is not error-proof. If you've purchased sexed chicks and some of them turned out to be roosters, most stores will offer a refund, but won't take the rooster back. Some farm or farm stores may buy back roosters. Refund and return policies differ from one place to another, so make sure to research that before purchasing chickens from a particular place.

If you've hatched your own eggs and ended with more roosters than you need or can keep, there are a few options you have for dealing with unwanted roosters.

You can try to re-home, sell, or trade unwanted roosters. That can be a challenge, as most people want chickens for eggs. There is a variety of places where you can advertise your offer, such as chicken meetups, local chicken communities, veterinary office, livestock auctions, and animal shelters. You can post an offer online, on Craigslist or Facebook groups, for example. Keep in mind, most people may be looking to take your rooster only to butcher it. There is nothing wrong with that, and you should decide for yourself if you're okay with that.

Another option is butchering the rooster. It may sound horrifying, especially if you're keeping chickens as pets. However, culling is a good skill to know because you may have to cull your chickens if they become sick and need to be put down. The best time to butcher a rooster is just when it starts crowing. You can do it yourself or take your rooster to an abattoir to butcher it for you. Even if your rooster is not particularly meaty, it will still make an excellent soup stock. If you don't want to eat your rooster yourself, you can make some pet food. Grind the meat, add some rice (for dogs, not for cats), cook it, make meal-sized portions, and freeze them.

Raising Chicks

We've just touched on the topic of raising chicks; however, I decided to reiterate the main points here, as this part may be useful if you're raising chicks bought from a hatchery.

Once your chicks have hatched, you'll need to feed them on starter feed. If the chicks have been naturally incubated by a hen, it's unlikely she'll leave her chicks much, so she can eat the starter feed too. When the chicks have grown a bit and are around 6 weeks old, you can allow them to mix with the other chickens in the coop, it's a good idea to do this at nighttime, when everyone is relaxed and wanting to go to sleep. Check on how they are getting along, and if any chickens are bullying the new chicks, then separate the chicks until they've grown more.

If you have hatched chicks in an incubator, then don't move them to a brooder until they have dried and look fluffy. You can make a brooder, with a heat lamp and food source, with pine shavings on the floor. Ensure it is ventilated and that each chick has a square foot of space. The temperature should be 93–95°F for the first week, then lower this by 3–5°F per week, for the first 6 weeks. After this time, they can be out of the brooder and you can move them in with the rest of your flock.

Ensure that chicks are in a covered run to stop any predators from attacking them. The mother hen will teach the chicks everything they need to know. Make sure that young chicks have food and water. You can dip their beaks in water gently to let them know where the water is, and you can do the same with food. If your brooder is lined with newspaper, you can scatter some feed on the floor, and chicks will eat it until they find the trough and get used to eating from it. You'll only need to do this for a few days until they get used to where the feeding troughs are. It's best to use red bulbs in a place with baby chicks so that if any chick has an injury, this won't show and cause other chicks to attack it. Make sure that waterers are very shallow for the chicks, and with pebbles in so that the chicks don't drown.

I remember when we bred chickens for the very first time. It was enormously rewarding and exciting seeing fluffy little chicks hatch out of the eggs and knowing that we had a part in this coming about. It's wonderful to see the creation of new animal lives, and we knew that they'd of course be wonderfully looked after in a free-range way, with plenty of space, good food, care, and love. We've not experienced any issues of hens picking on younger chicks, and we believe one of the key reasons for this is that our chicks and chickens are not overcrowded and have plenty of space.

Key takeaways from this chapter:

1. Think carefully about why you're breeding, whether this is for eggs, meat, show, or fun, as this may determine the type of hens you pick.

2. If you want a cockerel, do check the legal regulations to ensure you're allowed one at your property, and not just hens.

3. To help fertilize eggs, feed your hens a higher protein layer feed and oyster shell.

4. You can use starter chicken feed for broody hens who are hatching eggs.

5. Giving your hens vitamin A, D, and cod liver oil can be useful when breeding.

6. When you want to turn eggs, you can have them in an egg box, and raise an end of the egg box using a book.

7. Eggs tend to hatch within 21 days.

8. You can use a technique known as candling to see if an egg has been fertilized.

9. Ensure incubators are set to the correct temperature and humidity.

10. Clean incubators thoroughly after hatching.

11. Give chicks starter feed until they are 6 weeks old.

12. If you have incubated your chicks, move them to a brooder with the temperature of 93–95°F, and reduce this by 3–5°F per week for 6 weeks.

13. Have accessible food and water for chicks. You can scatter food on newspaper initially until they find the feeder; and have a shallow dish of water, preferably containing pebbles to prevent chicks from drowning.

The next chapter will look at egg production, identifying which of the hens are laying, and possible reasons why some may not, how to gather, clean, and store your eggs, and how to check them for quality. The chapter will also cover how you can preserve eggs.

Chapter 8: Egg Production

I adore eggs. I can't express how much I love them. Even above and beyond chocolate, there is something special about an egg. Eggs are so incredibly versatile and can be used in so many different ways as to how they're cooked, and in so many different recipes. My favorite way to cook an egg is to poach it, and I love it on a muffin, with hollandaise sauce. We as a family eat a lot of eggs and do a lot of baking with them. Egg production was one of our key purposes of getting chickens, as well as really enjoying them as pets with their own quirky and humorous personalities.

This chapter will cover everything you need to know about egg production. It will discuss how you can identify laying hens. It will let you know that hens can lay eggs without a rooster. It covers the reasons for why some hens may not lay, and what you can do to help encourage them to. It will discuss how to gather eggs, clean them, and store them.

This is a topic I am so passionate about, I can't wait to share my experiences with you so that you can get right into egg production, and know all the best tips and tricks, but avoid the mistakes I made initially.

Can Hens Lay Eggs without a Rooster?

It is a common misconception that hens won't lay eggs without a rooster. Hens will lay eggs once they are around 4–6 months old, depending on the breed. Their first eggs may be unusual shape or soft-shelled, but they'll soon get the hang of it and will start to produce good eggs. Eggs will be unfertilized if you don't have a rooster in your flock, so these eggs will never turn into a chick. There will be occasional hens who never lay an egg, but if they're healthy, this is rare.

If your hens have access to a rooster, you can still collect and eat the eggs, even if they are fertilized. Your eggs should be collected every day, to ensure freshness, and there is no possibility of finding a developing chick when you crack the egg open. There is no difference in taste or texture or nutrients between fertilized and unfertilized eggs. For an egg to turn into a chick, it would need to be either incubated by the hen sitting on it for 21 days, or being placed in an incubator for 21 days.

Identifying Laying Hens

So, you have your lovely chickens, but egg production is not that great. You're probably wondering—why is that? Some of your hens might be doing a great job of laying eggs, while others may not produce a thing. Here's how you can identify laying hens in order to find out which ones are not laying and what you can do to help encourage them to.

First things first, if you have young pullets, their point of lay (POL) can differ from breed to breed, but generally, pullets younger than 16 weeks are not yet ready to lay. You can find POL for your breed with a simple online search. Here are some signs that a pullet is approaching her POL:

- Her comb and wattles are getting larger and redder
- She becomes restless and moves from nest to nest, sort of looking for the "right spot"
- She starts squatting when you attempt to touch her
- She starts seeking out dark, quiet areas

- A rooster will start showing her some attention

Pullets who are approaching the POL will be active and alert, with bright eyes. They don't understand what's happening, and you may find their eggs in odd places, so keep an eye out. First eggs may be oddly shaped, and young pullets may not produce eggs regularly until they get used to it, which usually happens around 30 weeks or so.

As for adult hens older than a year, you can conduct a physical examination or resort to trap nesting.

Laying hens will have worn feathers, especially if you have a rooster in your flock. Their feathers may be broken or rumpled. That's because the calcium in her body is diverted to producing eggs, rather than feather making.

Often the combs and wattles on laying hens will be red. If they are dull and shrunken, it's highly likely the hen is not laying. For hens with yellow pigment, this will strengthen and lessen according to how much they are laying. You can also look to see how much fat a hen has around the abdomen. If the hen has a low amount of fat, it is more likely to be a laying hen. You can pick up your hens gently and look at their vents. A laying hen should have a clean, pink, and moist vent. If it's small, pale, and dry, the hen is not laying.

It may happen that all signs suggest your hens are laying, but you have few eggs, check to see they don't have a secret stash somewhere. Sometimes hens can lay eggs in odd places, especially if they are free range.

Trap nest is a device that is fitted to a nest box. It looks like a gate that shuts when a hen enters the nest box so that you can leave her there for a while and see if she's laying eggs. If you do that, don't leave your hens in the traps for a long time, especially in warm weather. They can get dehydrated, and they can simply get bored and eat their own eggs. It's a bad habit, and it's very contagious, you certainly don't want to promote it in your birds. I don't recommend trap nesting unless you've tried everything and still can't identify laying hens.

Why Hens May Not Lay

A hen will only lay one egg in a day, and there will be some days where she does not lay an egg. Once a hen has laid an egg, it takes typically 26 hours for an egg to form before it lays another. Hens need sunlight, and over the course of time, sometimes a hen will lay an egg too late in the day to start creating a new one because it's late and getting dark, so it will skip a day or two before it lays another egg.

Some hens will produce eggs for 3–4 years, but typically each year the egg production reduces. If your hens have been laying for 3–4 years previously, they may have reduced their egg laying.

If some of your hens are not laying, there are some things you can do to encourage them to. First of all, your chickens need to be well cared for in terms of what you feed them, the light they have access to, and their space, and entertainment. It's important that the feed the hens are getting has a good amount of nutrients and doesn't contain too much scratch grain. The diet also needs to be relevant for the type of hens you have—egg-laying hens will want a higher calcium diet compared to meat chickens or non-laying chickens. It is essential to check that your hens have fresh, clean water. During the winter months, you may need a water heater to stop the water from freezing over.

You need to have enough nesting boxes for everyone. Keep them clean and line them with some straw or pine shavings. You can try putting artificial eggs (often sold in feed stores) or golf balls into the nesting boxes to encourage laying behavior.

Chickens often stop laying due to stress. There are multiple factors that can contribute to increased stress of your chickens. Mishandling can stress out your birds really quick. Frightening them, holding them too tightly and/or in awkward poses can make them stressed out. Introducing new chickens to your flock can also be a stressful experience for your birds. If your chickens don't get enough time outside, they can become bored, which leads to more stress and them developing unfavorable habits, such as pecking at each other.

There are a few things you can do to relax and de-stress your flock. As mentioned previously, keep them well-fed and hydrated. Let your birds enjoy some fresh air whenever possible. You can add chicken swings and obstacles to keep them entertained. Lavender works wonders to help de-stress your chickens. You can put some lavender in their nesting boxes, which will help relax your birds and make your coop smell great too.

Happy, healthy hens will lay better quality eggs. Chickens will produce more eggs during the summer, when there is more sunlight, than in the darker winter months. If you have hens that you want to lay eggs all year round, then you need to ensure that they have 14 hours of light per day, you can use artificial lighting on a timer for this.

If your hen has been laying eggs for 10 months or more, they may have reached the end of the laying cycle. They will stop laying, will molt their feathers, have a break, then start laying again.

If nothing helps, you should check that your hens aren't infected with any parasites, as this can make them stressed, damage their health, and prevent them from laying eggs.

How to Stop Chickens from Eating Eggs

You may notice that hens can start eating their own eggs. This can become a huge problem once it takes hold. If you notice your chickens eating eggs—you need to stop this habit immediately. The longer they do it, the harder it becomes to break this unfavorable habit.

One of the main reasons hens start eating eggs is egg breakage. Preventing or at least minimizing egg breakage highly reduces the chance your hens will ever taste their eggs. If you find any broken eggs, you need to clean the area thoroughly and replace the bedding if necessary.

Here's what you can do to prevent egg breakage:

- You need one nesting box for every 4 hens in your flock. Nesting boxes should be at least 2 feet off the ground and at least 4 feet from the roosts.

- Keep at least 2 inches of fresh bedding material, such as wood shavings or straw, in the nesting boxes. This will provide additional padding and help prevent eggs from breaking.

- Broody hens should ideally be relocated away from the flock in the brooding box. This will help prevent congestion in the coop.

- Adding a calcium supplement, usually in the form of oyster shells, to your hens' diet can help make egg shells stronger, which in turn will make them harder to break. If you decide to feed your chickens egg shells, smash them to a powder so that your chickens don't associate them with eggs.

- Collect eggs early in the day, hens are typically done laying by 10 a.m.

Even though you've taken all possible precautions to prevent egg breakage, you may still find your chickens eating their eggs. This nasty habit is hard to break, but it's certainly possible. Here's what you can do to stop your chickens from eating their eggs:

- Overcrowding is one of the most common reasons chicken start eating their eggs. Make sure your chickens have 3–4 sq. ft. of space per chicken. If they don't, you need to give them more space. You'll have to either expand your coop or build a new one or reduce the number of chickens.

- As mentioned previously, if you don't have enough nesting boxes, this can cause heavy "traffic" to those boxes, which increases the chances of eggs getting trampled and cracked. You need 1 nesting box for every 4 hens. You can try adding a couple more even if you have enough already. Nesting boxes should be in dark areas of the coop, so make sure there isn't too much sunlight where they are. It may sound a bit silly, but you can add curtains to make the area darker, it does help tremendously.

- Your chickens can start eating eggs if they are hungry or thirsty, so fresh water and food should always be available for your flock. Some chickens can bully others and start guarding food and water. You can add more feeders and waterers so that all your chickens can eat and drink safely. Feed bought from feed stores is usually precisely formulated, so nutrient deficiencies are not that common in chickens. However, you should give them calcium supplement, which usually comes in the form of oyster shells, as a side dish.

- Sometimes chickens can simply get bored, especially if they don't have a lot of space outside and don't have any entertainment. You can add things like cabbage tetherball, rolling treat dispensers, and chicken swings to keep your chickens entertained and happy.

- Here's one technique I learned from my grandmother, it may seem a bit over the top, but it's incredibly effective and completely safe. Try this if nothing else works and your chickens keep breaking eggs and eating them. It's called "blowing eggs". Make small holes at the ends of an egg and blow out the contents. Put some mustard inside the empty egg shell, you can use a syringe to do that. Chickens hate the taste of mustard, so once they find this "surprise", this will stop them from breaking and eating eggs.

- You can also try ceramic eggs. It works well if the habit is ingrained and chickens have been eating eggs for quite some time. Chickens' beaks don't take well to hard objects, and there is no way they can break open ceramic eggs. Don't worry, your chickens won't break their beaks. However, after trying for some time to break open a ceramic egg, they will get tired and bored eventually, which should make them give up on trying to break eggs.

Gathering, Cleaning, and Storing Eggs

You want to make sure that the eggs you gather are clean and safe. It is good practice to gather eggs early in the morning, and if other commitments allow for it, to gather them twice a day. If you leave eggs too long or overnight, then eggs can get covered in poop, or become broken by being stood on. Having plenty of padding in the nesting boxes will help prevent eggs from breaking. You can use wood shavings or straw for this, and remember to keep your nesting boxes clean and replace the bedding regularly.

It is best to dry clean eggs because it keeps the eggs' outer layer, which is antibacterial, intact (the name for this layer is 'bloom'). When you dry clean, it simply means using something like a cloth, paper towel, sponge, loofah, or fine sandpaper to remove dirt and chicken poop from the egg.

If the eggs are very dirty, or have yolk on the shells, you may want to wet clean them. The water should be warmer than the egg, but not too hot, because otherwise this could partially cook the content of the egg and cause issues. Once you have wiped the eggs, dry them with a paper towel. You can sanitize the eggs with a tiny splash of bleach diluted in water. If you want to sell your eggs, it is worth checking the local and state regulations about cleaning eggs, to ensure that you comply with their safety standards.

When you store your eggs after cleaning them, it's best to keep them in egg cartons. Always put the date that you collected the eggs on the cartons and store them in the fridge. If you dry cleaned your eggs and the bloom is still intact, you can store them at room temperature, but they will last much longer in the fridge.

Egg Quality

Whilst there is no difference nutritionally between white-shelled and brown-shelled eggs, people often prefer to buy brown-shelled eggs, so this is something to keep in mind when picking your egg-laying breeds.

If you place an egg in water and it floats, this means there is now a big air pocket in the shell, the content of the egg has evaporated and spoiled. You can compost these eggs.

Different people will measure egg quality differently depending on whether the eggshell color is important to them or the freshness of an egg. People often want to know that the hens have been humanely treated, and some are interested in whether the hens have been fed organically. There is such a thing called the USDA grading system where eggs are graded.

Grade AA eggs are the highest quality eggs. They have thick and firm whites, high and round yolks that are practically free from defects, and clean, unbroken shells. Grade A eggs have characteristics of Grade AA eggs except that their whites are reasonably firm. This is the quality most often sold in stores. Grade B eggs have whites that are thinner and yolks that are wider and flatter than eggs of higher grades. Grade B eggs may have stains and if an egg doesn't have a typical egg shape, it will be downgraded to a Grade B egg. Grade B eggs are usually not sold in stores, and instead they find their way to bakers and food processors and are used to make liquid, frozen, and dried egg products.

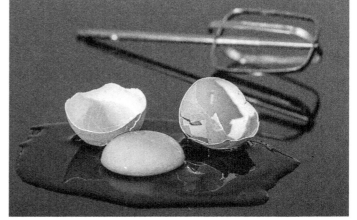

When people crack an egg open, the yolk should be round and in the center. If it is a flat yolk, off-center, then the chicken egg will not be fresh. Yolk color can be considered for quality and may depend upon the hen's diet and people's individual preferences.

Quality can also be determined by the size—many people prefer large and extra-large eggs. Eggs usually aren't carriers of salmonella, it's usually killed upon cooking, and if eggs ever do contain this, it's at incredibly small levels 2–5 milligrams, where it would take 100 to make a human sick from this. Salmonella is a rapidly multiplying bacteria, so it's important for eggs to be cooked thoroughly.

Preserving Eggs

Eggs should last for one month from the date that you collected them, provided you store them in the fridge. It could be that they are fine for a further 2 weeks after this. If you're using older eggs, you can use them in baking or make hard-boiled eggs.

Another technique you can use to preserve eggs is known as water glassing. So, if you have a plentiful supply of eggs that your hens have laid, and you want to keep them for when you know you may not have so many eggs, you can use water glassing. Advocates of water glassing claim that even after long periods of time, their eggs still taste as perfect as when they first collected them from their hens. There are different techniques you can use to water glass eggs, but the technique described below is very affordable and convenient. It uses hydrated lime, which comes under other names of 'pickling lime' or 'slacked lime' too. But it's all the same thing. When you use this method, it's a great way to store eggs throughout the winter, and even up to two years if you wanted, without needing to have them refrigerated.

I have mentioned that some people put artificial lighting in with the chickens for 14 hours a day to encourage them to keep laying. If this is your main livelihood by selling eggs, this may be something you wish to do. We personally take the approach of letting the hens decide when their bodies wish to lay eggs naturally, to keep them as healthy as possible. Our hens naturally lay more eggs in the summer than in the winter, so we do water glass some so that we have a ready supply of eggs when our hens aren't laying. If we reach a point where the hens are producing more eggs than we, as a family, can consume, and give away to family and friends or even sell at local markets, then we take that opportunity to preserve some of the eggs.

To preserve our eggs, we used hydrated lime, water (at room temperature) and some food storage containers. You can buy hydrated lime in bulk, 50 lb at a time, and this is affordable, and will last for years. Hydrated lime is natural, made of oyster shells, bones, and limestone. This is a different product to what you will find in an agricultural section of a hardware store, so do ensure you buy the right thing. Place your eggs that you have preserved in a cool part of your home, away from sunlight. They will definitely last 8 months to a year. Some people have said that even after two years their eggs are fine. You can't use washed eggs or store-bought eggs to water glass. You need to use fresh eggs you've collected that day and unwashed. Check that none of your eggs are floating.

The quantities you'll need to water glass an egg will include 8 oz of hydrated lime, 8 quarts of filtered water, and fresh collected eggs from your hens. Depending on how many eggs you want to preserve will dictate the size of container you use. You need enough water and lime solution to completely cover your eggs. For every quart of water, you will use an ounce of lime. Keep this ratio up for whatever size of container you decide to use. Ensure constantly throughout the preserving process that the water hasn't evaporated leaving your eggs uncovered, so either cover the container with a lid to prevent evaporation, or you can add a layer of olive oil on the top of the water, and just keep checking. If possible, position your eggs small side down. When you are ready to use them, remove, rinse, and use them how you would typically use an egg.

You may find that the container smells a little, but not rotten, and this is nothing to worry about. You may notice that some of the lime settles, this is just because it's heavier than water, and you don't need to worry about this either, and you don't need to stir it back in. This technique doesn't 'pickle' your eggs. The end result is raw, usable eggs.

The lime solution can dry out the skin on your hands, so it's best to wear gloves during this process. Take precautions not to inhale the lime powder. Provided you don't deliberately sniff it, it should not be harmful to you.

Wash each egg before you use it after preserving. Remember we spoke earlier about an egg's natural protective layer called 'bloom'. This will protect the egg all the time it is being preserved from the lime, which is why you shouldn't wash them prior to preserving. The eggs you have preserved should taste no different to a normal egg, for up to 8 months of preserving, after this time, they're better for baking than frying.

I still remember when I collected eggs for the first time, as a child at my grandmother's; and I remember too, the first time as an adult with our own chickens. Our family loves having fresh eggs daily, and we always give fresh eggs to friends, family, and neighbors. Anytime someone comes to visit, we give them some fresh eggs to take away, or some produce that we've baked with our delicious eggs. Our eggs are of an amazing quality. The yolks are rich, tasty, and lovely deep yellow. They're incredible eggs to soft-boil and dip soldiers into, or to poach, or have scrambled, and they make amazingly fluffy Victoria sponge cakes too. Our friends and family, who we have shared eggs with, do say that they taste so much better than eggs bought from a supermarket. The chickens and their eggs have been raised with love, and you can taste it in the wonderful produce.

Key takeaways from this chapter:

1. You can identify laying hens by their red combs and wattles, or how their yellow pigmentation varies, also a low amount of fat indicates a laying hen.

2. Chickens can lay eggs without a rooster, they just won't be fertilized, and will never become a chick.

3. For a fertilized egg to become a chick, it needs incubating by a hen sitting on it for 21 days or placing it in an incubator for 21 days.

4. Sometimes hens may not lay eggs just simply due to the time it takes to form and lay an egg. Hens also need sunlight for egg laying. It could be past their production time of 3–4 years, and they may have slowed down laying. Another reason could be that if they've laid for 10+ months, they've reached the end of their laying cycle, they'll molt, have a break, and lay again when they're ready. Hens can stop laying if they are not well-fed and hydrated and if they're stressed. Another reason can be to check that the hens aren't infected with any parasites as this can impact their health and make them not lay.

5. Hens need good food, light, space, entertainment, and fresh water to be happy to lay. Also ensure that egg-layers have calcium via oyster shell.

6. It is possible to encourage more laying via artificial light for 14 hours per day if you choose to. We prefer to let the hens lay naturally and feel this is healthier.

7. You can gather eggs, ideally early, and if possible, twice a day.

8. If you can dry-clean eggs to protect the outer layer (known as bloom) this is best.

9. You can wet-clean very dirty eggs, but this is less preferable.

10. Store cleaned eggs in the fridge in an egg carton with their collection date clearly visible.

11. Eggs that float have large air pockets and may have spoiled.

12. You can preserve eggs with the water glassing technique with hydrated lime. Use 1 ounce of hydrated lime per quart of filtered water.

The next chapter will look at raising chickens for meat. Chicken is a wonderfully versatile meat to cook with, soaking up any flavors you put with it. It's wonderful roasted, it's great in a curry, great poached and shredded with BBQ sauce, lovely in wraps with a peri spice rub. We eat a lot of chicken every week, more than any other meat, because of its versatility. The next chapter will cover what you should feed meat birds (including corn feed, which gives the chicken a lovely golden color and richer taste). It will look at health issues that can occur with broiler chickens. It will discuss when best to butcher birds and how to butcher them. It will cover how you should store poultry in a sanitized and safe manner.

Chapter 9: Raising Chickens for Meat

Chicken as meat is so incredibly versatile it's become the staple meat for many families. There is such a wide variety of meals you can do with it: roast dinners, curries, chicken stuffed with cheese topped with pesto, hunter's chicken (with bacon, cheese and BBQ sauce), chicken fillet burgers with crisp iceberg lettuce and mayo, sweet n' sour chicken with noodles, garlicky chicken kievs, lemon and black pepper chicken, chicken chasseur with a lovely creamy sauce, sticky chicken skewers or sate ones and much more. The meat is tasty on its own, in sandwiches, or as part of a salad, but the meat also isn't so overpowering in its taste which makes it a great meat for taking on the flavors of whatever you decide to pair it with. It's a wonderful non-fatty lean meat, which is pretty healthy for you to eat, provided you don't always have it fried.

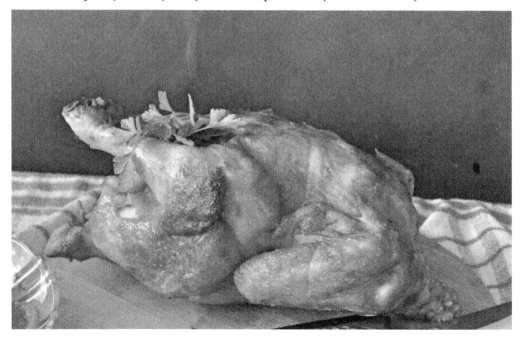

This chapter will focus on raising chickens for meat. It will look at what you should feed the birds intended to be used for meat. It will discuss health issues that can occur with broiler chickens that you need to look out for. The chapter will discuss when and how you should butcher a meat chicken. Finally, the chapter will conclude with how to store poultry safely.

It is worth considering if this is something that you really think you want to do before starting. You may need to raise a lot of chickens, you will deal with a lot of chicken poop, and eventually you will need to slaughter the chickens, so you need to consider if this is something you want to deal with, and can emotionally handle before starting.

Treat your chickens humanely for the time they're alive. They will want roosts, but not too high, because you don't want them to hurt or break their legs. These chickens will carry more weight than egg-laying chickens. Just like egg-laying chickens they will want dust baths to stay cool, but when they grow large, they can't always kick enough dust over themselves, so you could provide a sprinkler, lots of fresh water, and shade to keep them cool.

Feeding Meat Chickens

You should feed your chicks with medicated starter feed for the first 3 weeks and then give them feed which is called 'grower' or finishing feed. This type of food has more protein in it. During week 1 your chicks should have access to food all day long. However, from week 2 it's time to change the feeding schedule. They should have access to food for 12 hours a day, and then not have any access to food during the other 12 hours. It's better to give them food during the day, as chickens are creatures of habit and are used to eating during the day. How much you need to feed your chickens depends on their breed; however, feeding plans for broilers are quite similar. Here is a sample feeding plan intended for Cornish Crosses which can be used for other breeds with a few small tweaks:

- Week 1: 5 ounces starter feed per week
- Week 2: 11 ounces starter feed per week
- Week 3: 1 pound grower feed per week
- Week 4: 1.5 pounds grower feed per week
- Week 5: 2.5 pounds grower feed per week
- Week 6 to slaughter, 3 pounds grower feed per week

When feeding your chickens, watch for signs of exhaustion or inability to move. If you notice they are overfed, and it's difficult for them to get to the waterer, reduce their feed consumption by 5% until they appear more lively. Broilers are typically lazy, but if you notice that it's hard for them to move and even get to a waterer—this is a clear sign they're overfed and you need to reduce their feed intake slightly for some time until they become more lively.

Their water should be on the opposite side of the pen to the food, and it should always be clean and fresh and available at all times. It means they have to walk to the other side of the pen to get their water, and get some exercise to develop muscle, and not become too lazy.

If you are letting your chickens feed organically from your land, it may take longer for them to grow, and you could need to wait between 6 months to a year for your chickens to be ready.

As mentioned previously, broilers are known for being a bit lazy, and they may lay in their feeders, so it's best to keep feeders off the ground, to avoid poop near the food and bacteria growing.

Broiler Health Issues

Some commercial chickens grow very large, even abnormally so, and this can mean that the chicken's legs can't support its body, which can lead to heart and respiratory issues. The chickens' bodies are simply not able to carry the weight that they put on so quickly, and some may even have heart attacks.

The official term for heart failure and a build-up of fluid in the stomach and lungs is called 'Ascites', and you may recognize this if the birds appear out of breath, or if their combs have a bluish tinge. Having well ventilated chicken housing can lower the likelihood of this occurring. You can check that your broilers don't have any issues with their legs by ensuring they can move around fine, and checking to see that they don't have any leg or back deformities. Always check that your chickens are eating and drinking properly.

Some broilers who have previously seemed fine can keel over with sudden death syndrome. This typically tends to happen between 2 and 4 weeks old, and no explanation is currently known for why this occurs.

It is possible to slow down the pace of broiler chicken's growth, and by doing so, this can prevent such illnesses occurring, this can be done in the first three weeks of a broiler's life by giving them feed twice a day, rather than offering them feed all day long. Another option is to remove food overnight, and give birds food for 12 hours, but then leave them without food for 12 hours.

When to Butcher Broilers

Different breeds of chicken mature at different times, and other things that can impact the time when your chicken should be butchered can depend on how often you feed them and the type of feed. It's useful to research the breed of chicken that you have so that you are aware of its growth rate, and what size it should be when it has finished growing. This will help you to know when the chickens should be slaughtered. You will need to consider the chicken's weight and the chicken's age.

As previously mentioned, one of the most common broiler birds is the Cornish Cross Broiler, they grow large and fast. It is sensible when you buy this type of bird to have a predetermined date in mind, for when your birds will be slaughtered because if they grow too large, then they will start to develop health issues. If you have Cornish Cross chickens, you will need to slaughter them within 8–9 weeks. There are also Ranger breeds, and they usually require butchering around 10 weeks.

If you have picked heritage breeds, it could be much longer before you need to butcher your chicken, anything from 6 months to a year depending on the breed, for example, something like a Jersey Giant. For heritage breeds, it could be a good idea to wait until your chicken has reached a certain weight before butchering. You could butcher it up to 10 months old, without the chicken being too tough. The longer you leave a chicken, the tougher the meat will be, but if you intend to use it for soup or in a slow cooker, this won't matter to you too much. Heritage chickens will look quite different to your typical Cornish Cross, which typically has white meat. Heritage chickens have more yellow-colored meat, and their bodies are more bony.

How to Butcher Broilers

It's one of the more unpleasant jobs connected to raising chickens for meat. However, you know that when you get broilers, you're not keeping these chickens as pets, and that they have a relatively short lifespan. It is a necessity that needs doing because the chickens would develop health conditions if they weren't butchered. Often people tend to cull chickens at the end of fall, for a number of reasons. Chickens, as discussed earlier, will lay fewer eggs during the winter, because daylight hours are shorter, but they still need to eat as much food during this time, which can cost more, with little income from them. The fewer birds you have over winter, the less chance there will be for illness. Also, the birds provide valuable meat which can be used to feed your family.

Whilst you can butcher chickens yourself, my advice would be to take them to an abattoir, so this is done for you. If you want to do it yourself, you'll need to prepare the birds and processing area first. The night before you butcher the birds, don't feed them so that their crop is empty.

Here is the equipment that you'll need:

- I highly recommend using a kill cone, as it will prevent the birds from flopping around; however, you can use an axe if you're comfortable with that

- If you're using an axe, you'll also need a chopping block, you can use a large round stump

- A sharp boning knife

- Poultry shears (to remove head)

- Scalding tank—it makes plucking so much easier

- Automatic chicken plucker if you have access to one, or you can pluck the birds manually, it's not too difficult

- Hose for rinsing the processing area and equipment

- Stainless steel table for processing

- Garbage cans or buckets for guts, blood, and feathers
- Ice chest with ice to put finished chickens in
- Bags for feet and hearts
- Thermometer for measuring scalding tank temperature

Once everything is ready, you'll need to catch your chickens, you could use a net to help. If you're using an axe, make sure to sharpen it beforehand. Grab the chicken by its feet. It will instinctively stick its head out. Make a clean swing to sever the head. The chicken will start flopping, don't worry, it's just a natural reflex and they are not alive when this happens. Place the chicken on the ground and wait until it stops flopping. You've successfully culled the chicken at this point.

If you're using a kill cone, place the chicken's head in the cone facing head down. Bring the chicken's head down and slice just below the jaw line into the jugular, an artery. As soon as the blood starts draining, the chicken will pass out and die. Allow the blood to drain for a couple of minutes and then cut the head off, you can use poultry shears to do that. Wait a few more minutes to allow all of the blood to drain.

20

---

[20] Image from Melissa Knorris: https://melissaknorris.com/podcast/how-to-butcher-chickens-part-2-of-raising-meat-chickens/

Once the bird has been culled, you need to decide whether to pluck or skin it. IF you decide to pluck it, suggest using a scalding tank. Start boiling the water to 150°F–160°F before you start culling the chickens so that the tank is ready once you've culled them. Take the chicken by its feet and put it in headfirst to wet the feathers for 1–2 minutes. You can use hooks to hang

up the chickens instead of holding them. Don't leave it too long because you don't want to start cooking the chicken. Check to see if the feathers are coming out easily, and if they are—the chicken is ready for plucking. This whole process can be quite stinky, so it's better to do it on a colder day if possible.
21

Now it's time to pluck the chicken. You can use a mechanical chicken plucker that will remove the feathers and rinse the chicken at the same time; however, it can be quite costly. You can pluck the chicken yourself, of course. Just grab the feathers and pull them out. If there are hairs left after plucking, you can run a blowtorch over the chicken to remove them.[22]

21 Image from The Prairie Homestead: https://www.theprairiehomestead.com/2016/07/how-to-butcher-a-chicken.html

22 Image from The Prairie Homestead: https://www.theprairiehomestead.com/2016/07/how-to-butcher-a-chicken.html

If you decide to skin the bird instead of pluck it, then you'll need to spray the chicken down and then start making slits around the feet. Then cut down to its groin and pull the skin down towards its head.

Next, you'll need to cut the feet. I suggest cutting at the valley of the joint as it will help you avoid the bones and make a quick cut. Hitting the bones will dull your knife. You can save the feet for chicken stock if you'd like.

23

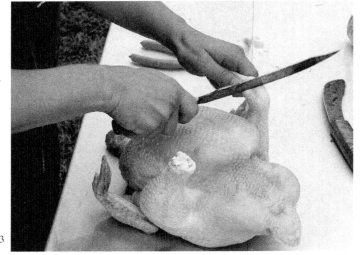

Now you need to remove the oil gland. Place the chicken breast side down and push the tail up so the oil gland is sticking up. Cut it off with the knife. If you don't, it will taint the taste of the meat.

24

---

23 Image from Melissa Knorris: https://melissaknorris.com/podcast/how-to-butcher-chickens-part-2-of-raising-meat-chickens/

24 Image from Melissa Knorris: https://melissaknorris.com/podcast/how-to-butcher-chickens-part-2-of-raising-meat-chickens/

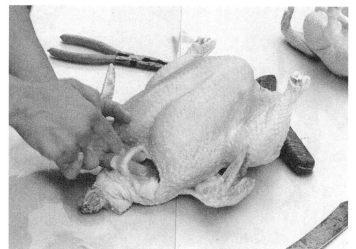

The chicken will then need gutting. Make a slice at the base of the neck above the breastbone. Find the crop, windpipe, and esophagus and pull your fingers behind the windpipe and esophagus and bring them out, then break the connective tissue at the crop. Don't pull this assembly out completely yet.

25

With the chicken laying on its back, flip it 180 degrees to work on the back end. Make a cut above the vent and tear open the carcass with your hands.

26

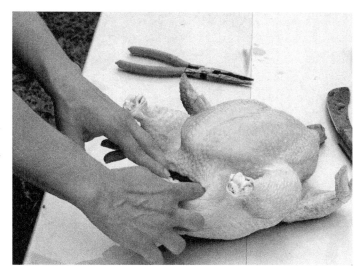

---

25 Image from Melissa Knorris: https://melissaknorris.com/podcast/how-to-butcher-chickens-part-2-of-raising-meat-chickens/

26 Image from Melissa Knorris: https://melissaknorris.com/podcast/how-to-butcher-chickens-part-2-of-raising-meat-chickens/

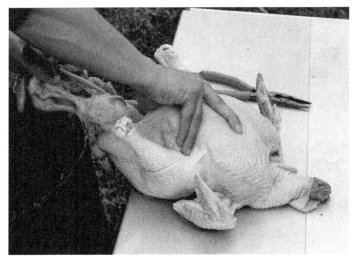

Now put your hand into the carcass, pull the fat off the gizzard, and hook your finger around the esophagus. Pull it all out, you should have a bunch of connected organs. Cut down either side of the vent and underneath in order to remove all the guts. Finally, remove the lungs and windpipe and anything else that didn't come out. [27]

After doing this, you'll need to rinse the bird and ensure that all water coming off is clean. You can make a slice in the excess skin that's hanging off the back cavity and then tuck the legs up through the hole so you have a nice little package.

Storing Poultry

Once your birds have been killed, plucked/skinned and gutted, you'll need to get them ready for cooking with or storing. Quartering birds can make them easy to work with. If you place a knife in joint sockets, they will easily come apart. You need to chill the chickens before storing them. So, once you've gutted and washed them, put the chicken in a cooler filled with ice or in the fridge for 16–24 hours.

You can keep freshly butchered chicken for up to a week in a refrigerator, but it should be on a plate, and covered with wax paper or freezer paper rather than tightly wrapped in plastic.

You can freeze whole chickens, as well as half or quarter chicken in freezer bags, depending on how you cut them up. Make sure you have all the air out of the freezer bag, then place in the freezer. Some people dry the carcass inside and out before freezing it. Some people will also double-bag if the plastic is thin. If you're going to be freezing a lot of chicken, you

---

[27] Image from Melissa Knorris: https://melissaknorris.com/podcast/how-to-butcher-chickens-part-2-of-raising-meat-chickens/

could contemplate vacuum heat sealers because these would keep your chicken preserved for longer.

If you choose to do so, and many people are opting to use as many parts of an animal as possible, you may choose to keep things like feet, head, neck, skin, and bones for a stock pot. Some people may decide to cook the liver, heart, and gizzard. Even if you don't wish to use these parts yourself, another option is to give them to your pets, or other farm animals, to give them more protein. If you have too many to use at once, then you can pop them into freezer bags.

There is such a wide variety of ways you can cook with chicken, from delicious chicken pies with leek and ham hock, chicken casseroles, chicken curry, a roast dinner, chicken buns, fried chicken, and much, much more.

Key takeaways from this chapter:

1. Broiler chickens usually reach 10 lb by 10 weeks old.

2. Bresse chickens are some of the best tasting in the world, they're a bit more pricey, but worth it.

3. Cornish Cross chickens are the most well-known meat chickens.

4. Other types of meat chickens include Freedom Rangers and the Jersey Giant.

5. To help your meat chickens develop muscle, put the water on the opposite side to their food, to get them walking between them.

6. You should feed meat chickens with grower or finishing feed because it contains more protein.

7. Broilers can develop health issues, where their legs can't support them, and they get heart or respiratory issues.

8. A tip is to slow down feeding in the first three weeks of a broiler's life, as this will help them not to grow too quickly, and possibly prevent them from having health issues.

9. When you should butcher a chicken, does depend on its breed and weight, but typically it will be 8–9 weeks, and before 10 weeks for most breeds. When you butcher a chicken, this should be done humanely, and as quickly as possible.

10. When plucking a chicken, if you dunk its feathers in hot water a few times, it will make feathers come out much easier.

11. You can easily freeze whole or quartered chickens in the freezer.

The next chapter will look at putting chickens to work in your garden, discussing the variety of ways that you can use chickens, looking at pest control, and using chicken manure to fertilize plants and vegetables.

Chapter 10: Putting Chickens to Work in the Garden

So, if you're thinking about raising chickens, or perhaps have recently purchased some, you will most likely have considered that you can gain eggs from them or use them for meat. But did you know how incredibly useful chickens can be to help you with your garden? I'll admit it wasn't the first thing that sprang to mind when we first got our chickens. Chickens will thoroughly enjoy being in your garden, and the space, exercise, and variety in their diet will be excellent for them. It will also give them a source of entertainment and make their lives more fulfilled. But they can also help you to prep your garden, clean it up, till your crops, and fertilize your soil!

This chapter will cover the many different ways that you can use your chickens to help you in the garden. They are fantastic at eating grubs and insects, which would otherwise feed on your plants and vegetables, so they can do great natural pest control, allowing you to grow organically without the need for unhealthy and environmentally unfriendly pesticides. They also naturally produce chicken manure, which is an excellent fertilizer for your garden.

Ways to Use Your Chickens in the Garden

You need to be sensible about when and where you use chickens in your garden. If you place chickens in a vegetable garden that is abundant with peppers, tomatoes, and lettuce, then clearly that's too much for the chickens to resist and they are going to eat them! It is essential to set up barriers so that the chickens work on the areas of the garden that you want them to, and avoid the areas you don't want them to touch. You can use temporary fencing to barricade off any areas you don't want them to scratch, peck, and eat. Or you could use a chicken tractor to move your chickens around the garden to the areas you want them to work on. If you're going to use a chicken tractor, and you're making it yourself, a top tip is to keep it as light as possible so that you can easily move it around your garden where you need it. There is more information about chicken tractors in Chapter 3 of the book, which covers chicken housing.

Chickens don't know what you want them to do in the garden, and how much work you have put in. Their behavior is natural. So, chickens will eat seeds that you've sewn, they will pull up newly sprouted seedlings, which is fine if it's a weed, but obviously not so good if it's a plant or vegetable you've lovingly grown. They will take a dust bath in an area you've painstakingly tilled and will cover any vegetation in soil. They will strip plants of their leaves and flowers. They'll help themselves to fruits and vegetables. They're not doing this to be deliberately destructive, but just because it's their natural behavior and they are excited about the food, so this is why it is essential to securely fence off all areas that you don't want them to have access to.

So, if you're not prepared to spend some time and money fencing off the garden or using a chicken tractor, perhaps only give your chickens access to the garden when all your plants have ended and you want some help with cleaning up. You can zone your garden with plants that tend to ripe around the same time. For example, you could place peppers and tomatoes together, and squash that comes later could be placed in a different zone. This will allow you to move the chickens around the vegetable zones accordingly and make life easier for you. It is worth noting that chickens often don't stay in areas that they should, so if your chickens do not have their wings clipped, they may not stay in the areas you have fenced off. Smaller and inexperienced, such as young bantams, are usually easier to manage around the garden. Whereas a more mature five-year-old Australorp, for example, can be harder to manage.

It is generally best to place egg-laying chickens in your garden to work for you, or dual-purpose chickens. Meat chickens, like the Cornish Cross, lose interest in foraging as they gain weight. Birds like Wyandotte, Leghorn, and Australorp are excellent birds to help you in the garden. Broody hens may make a nest and be hard to move, so be aware of this. It's best to leave chicks out of an overgrown garden environment. Even if you don't wish to put your chickens in the garden, you can give them grubs you find, as well as weeds and rotted fruits.

Some people let their chickens follow behind the garden tiller, to eat up any squirming bugs that happen to have been turned up. But you can allow the chickens to till the ground for you by scratching instead. There are things that chickens naturally do that can be used to great benefit in your garden. Chickens feet are like mini rakes, and they can tear apart debris, till soil, aerate organic matter, spread compost, or mulch for you. The hens will be scratching about looking for food, but this can be a great help to you in the garden. One chicken alone can till 50 square feet of established sod in 4–6 weeks. They're much more environmentally friendly than a machine tiller because they don't require any fossil fuel to run, and they're much quieter too.

If you want to spread compost at the base of a tree or a bush, tip it there, and your hens will naturally spread that out for you. If you want straw on your garden beds, put it at the side, and the hens will spread it for you. They really are a great help and can save you quite some time.

Chickens spend a lot of time pecking the ground, and they like little bits of plants. If you use your chickens in the garden in early spring, they will do a ton of weeding for you and perhaps save you needing to hoe.

Chickens love dust baths, if the ground is dry and you want to add things like rock phosphate and greensand into your garden, sprinkle it over the surface of garden beds, and your chickens will mess up all the soil, which will mix in the aggregate and they will get an enjoyable dust bath at the same time.

One technique you could employ is to plant cover crops. It's a great way to feed your chickens naturally and to enrich your soil. Things like peas are perfect for planting in early spring or late fall. Chickens also like alfalfa, clover, rape, turnips, millet, flax, buckwheat, ryegrass, and kale. You could create a mix to plant.

Another way to use chickens to help in your garden is to add organic matter to your soil, such as dried leaves, mulch, wood chips, and straw. Chickens love to tear apart straw bales and spread them over the garden, and piles of woodchips too. If you want to start the chickens off, you could put a handful of chicken scratch on each pile of straw or wood chips that you want them to spread. It keeps the chickens active, entertained, and having fun. Happy chickens are healthy chickens! Chickens will also help you turn compost piles. A flock of 30 chickens will spread a large pile of leaves in half a day, and a cubic yard of compost in a couple of weeks.

Chickens can dispose of what we consider to be trash. Chickens will eat various food scraps we'd throw out. This gives them a varied diet, helps reduce waste, and they convert this "trash" into eggs or meat!

Once your garden has finished growing season, you can let your chickens run free through the garden eating up any leftover vegetables, such as zucchini and green tomatoes, they'll have an enjoyable time and will enrich their diet, and you won't have as much cleaning up to do!

If you have a patch of lawn that you'd like to turn into a vegetable garden, get your hens to do the work. You could fence the area off to prevent other animals from getting in. The hens will eat the grass, scratch up the soil, and make the area ready for planting. They will naturally fertilize the soil for new plants. You could place compost on the area and plant it with vegetables accordingly.

Pest Control

Chickens will eat bugs as they go through your garden, which is a great and very natural form of pest control without insecticide, pesticides, or other chemicals. Chickens will also get rid of slugs that can ruin your plants and vegetables. Chickens love grasshoppers too, and things like scorpions, termites, mice, flies, and June bugs. Chickens will eat things like Colorado potato beetles before they make it into the garden. They will also eat asparagus beetles, Japanese beetles, and Mexican bean beetles. Chickens can reduce ticks on homesteads and prevent the spread of Lyme Disease. Chickens will get rid of aphids for you too.

One chicken can de-bug up to 120 square feet a week. They will eat beetles, insects, and grubs. They will scratch down into the soil for 6 inches or more. A flock of 15 chickens could clear a 1800 square foot space in a week or so.

Chickens are great at de-bugging orchards and getting rid of insects there. They can really help with how much fruit your orchard can produce, once it's a bug-free zone. It can be a good idea to have your chickens there in the spring when worms lay their eggs, and perhaps in the fall to deal with fallen fruit, but you don't want them there all the time, as chickens poop a lot, and fruit trees tend to not want too much nitrogen.

The only bug they don't tend to touch is squash bugs, but if you want to get rid of them, you can use soapy water. It won't cause harm to your chickens eating other bugs.

Composting and Using Chicken Manure

Chicken manure is one of the best things in the world to place on a vegetable garden, it's an excellent fertilizer. It is high in nitrogen and also contains potassium and phosphorus. You do need to properly compost the manure first because raw manure can kill and burn roots. When you compost the manure, it breaks down the nutrients and mixes them with carbon too, to create the perfect compost.

To start composting chicken manure, you'll need a compost bin. The manure you scrape out of the coop is usually mixed with things like kitchen scraps, soiled bedding, plant debris, leaves, small sticks, and paper. Chicken poop in rich in nitrogen, so I suggest mixing 1 part of manure to 2 parts of other materials mentioned previously, such as soiled bedding, kitchen scraps, leaves, small sticks, and paper. You'll need at least one cubic foot of material to allow the composting process to start so that the pile can heat up to an internal temperature of 140°F to 160°F, which will kill pathogenic bacteria. Compost needs moisture, so add some water until the compost pile has the texture of a wet sponge.

Now you need to monitor the temperature of your compost pile. You can use a composting thermometer which you can buy at a home-improvement store or online. The goal is to reach the internal temperature of 140°F to 160°F and maintain it for 3 days. It will help kill salmonella and common bacterial pathogens found in chicken manure. Now the internal part has been treated; however, the outside has not, so you need to turn the compost pile. Turning the compost pile allows fresh air to enter and the good bacteria need some fresh air to continue working. Use a shovel or garden fork to move the center out to the sides and pull the sides into the center to repeat the heating process. Considering you clean your coop weekly, you will be adding more chicken manure and composting materials to the pile every week. You'll need to turn the compost pile every 3 days until it is full. When it's full, it needs to rest covered in order to cure for at least 80 days. It can take 6–9 months for chicken manure to be properly composted. When it's ready, there shouldn't be any unpleasant smells, it should be dark, and have the texture of good soil. Now you can spread it over the garden, and work it into the soil. Your vegetables will grow much bigger and healthier.

If you are planning on creating compost piles, keep in mind they may smell. Of course, it's highly likely your neighbors will not appreciate this. If your manure smells, it may not have enough air, so you need to turn the compost pile more frequently, and it should smell earthy.

Chicken manure will naturally accumulate in your chicken coop, and on the land. You can't just leave it in the coop—it's unhygienic, it smells, and will attract pests, plus the ammonia in it is not good for you or your chickens to inhale. So, it is good to compost it so that your soil contains more organic matter, holds water better, and has healthier bacteria in the soil. It will provide more of the good nutrients to your soil than horse or cow manure. It can be beneficial when you're composting to alternate layers of nitrogen (chicken poop) and carbon (straw, hay, wood chippings, cardboard etc.) and add water to this, and turn it, to help it to compost quicker.

We went through a couple of summers where chafer bugs decimated the lawns of our gardens. We let the chickens onto the grass, and they ate all the chafer bugs, and scratched the grass. This was perfect to lay some fresh grass seed and our grass has looked lovely ever since!

Our garden grows beautiful flowers and vegetables, and I truly believe this is in large part due to our chickens. Not only do they control and eat all the pests in the garden, so they can't damage our flowers and vegetables, we also have lots of chicken manure, which is rich in nutrients that help enrich our soil. Our plants grow bigger and have healthier fruit which taste amazing. It really helps us live a more sustainable lifestyle.

Key takeaways from this chapter:

1. Put barriers and fences up to cordon off the areas that you don't want your chickens scratching, pecking, and eating. Or you could use a chicken tractor.

2. Zone your garden produce so that things that produce at the same time are together, and this will make it easier to use chickens in different sections of your garden.

3. Egg-layers and dual-purpose chickens are the best to help in your garden.

4. Chickens can till the ground via scratching, and this is more environmentally friendly.

5. You can spread compost, mulch, or straw at the base of trees or on garden beds using chickens who will spread this for you.

6. Chickens can do the weeding for you, especially in the springtime.

7. Chickens will enjoy using dust baths and could help mix in aggregate into the soil at the same time.

8. You can use chickens to help you add organic matter, dried leaves, mulch, wood chips, and straw into soil.

9. Chickens can eat scraps and help to dispose of household waste.

10. Chickens can tidy up after any veg crops.

11. Chickens can turn lawn areas into vegetable plots.

12. Chickens provide great pest control of bugs, slugs, grasshoppers, termites, aphids, beetles, ticks, snails, and more. They can de-bug orchards, which will make them produce more fruit in the future.

13. Chicken manure is an excellent fertilizer. It is best to compost this so that the nitrogen doesn't burn plant roots.

The next chapter will look at creating a business out of your chickens, making money and profit from them, rather than them just being pets, or simply for your own use. It will look at different sectors you can focus on, such as eggs, meat, breeding, or a combination of these. It will look at the egg sale and chicken breeding business, both in terms of the law, market research, creating a business plan, costs, quantities of chicken, and marketing your produce. It will help you to determine if this is a viable option for you.

Chapter 11: Chicken Farming Business

If you're contemplating making a sustainable income from chickens, this can be a wonderful idea. Chickens are multipurpose, and can be used for eggs, meat, as dual-purpose chickens, or to breed chicks. They can also give you amazing fertilizer. Chickens don't cost that much to buy, their upkeep is not very expensive, and they grow quickly. Raising poultry is a fast-growing part of agriculture, so there can be some competition too, which you need to be aware of. Figures from the USDA show that this is a robust industry even during the pandemic: the combined value of production from broilers, eggs, turkeys, and the value of sales from chickens in 2020 was $35.5 billion, down 11 percent from $40.0 billion in 2019. Egg production in this same year was up, in terms of value.

Raising your own chicks on the property is an incredible thing. It's so nice to see them grow and start producing eggs. That is incredible in itself. But the moment you get people paying for boxes of the eggs that your hens have produced under your care, it's a kind of surreal moment! It's enormously rewarding, not just financially (though that too), but knowing that people enjoy how delicious your hens' eggs are, and comment on their luscious dark yellow yolk, and come back week after week requesting more, and taking other boxes for their friends and family. It makes it all worthwhile, and gives a great sense of achievement that you've done a great job in raising your chickens, giving them the best food, living conditions, supplements, and care. What an incredible way to make an extra income!

This chapter will look at having chickens for business purposes in order to make a profit from them and create a more sustainable lifestyle. Firstly, the chapter will look at whether you want to focus on the egg, meat, or breeding sector, or a combination of those. It will then look at each of the businesses, and consider what the law says, market research, making a business plan, determining costs, quantities of chickens that you would require for your business endeavor, and how you would market your produce. It's an exciting chapter for those seriously considering creating a business out of chickens and making a more sustainable lifestyle for themselves out of a smallholding. It's a natural progression really, from having chickens solely for your own use, to gradually expanding this as a business to make some income from. Once you have everything in place for your own chickens in terms of a coop, runs, food, and water, it doesn't take much more to add a few extra chickens, provided you have the space, and to ramp up your production.

Choosing Your Sector

You need to decide which aspect of the chicken farming business you would like to enter into, whether that's selling eggs, selling chickens for meat, breeding chickens to sell or show, or a combination of these. It could be that you've started small and have some chickens that provide your family and friends with eggs, and you'd like to scale up and do this as a full-time business.

Whatever business you want to start with chickens, there are four key strategic steps you need to take to ensure that your business will be viable. Start out by studying and understanding your market, this is key for any business in the world. Next, check the laws that apply to you in your state or country regarding selling eggs, meat, or breeding chickens. It's essential that you research this thoroughly so that you don't break any laws, and comply with everything you need to right from the start. The third step is to put together a marketing and business plan, so think about numbers, costs, scaling up, and how you will advertise your product to people, to ensure that you have sales and regular customers. Another good reason for putting together a business plan, is so that should your business do very well and you wish to expand in the future, having a business plan can help potential investors in your business know that your business is solid and worth investing in. A business plan can include an industry overview, executive summary, products, mission and vision statement, jobs you'll create, target market, and pricing strategy. If you are looking at a larger scale operation, you will need to consider the cost of staff salaries. If you're just planning to do this on a smaller scale from your home, you may want to think about whether you need to invest in any more land.

The final step involves planning how many chicks or chickens you require for your business. You may want a name for your business, a web page, and a logo that you can put on all your products. When you first start out, you don't need to spend vast amounts of money on a website or logo, you can hire a freelancer to create a logo for you on the cheap, for example, on Fiverr or Upwork. And you can set up a free website at first with very little technical knowledge, for example using Wix or Squarespace. Make sure the website is easy to navigate, fast, and updated with the latest info.

One of the best things you can do, if you wish to go into the chicken business, is network with people. The more people you tell about your business, the more people will know where to come when they want eggs, meat, or chicks. Try to attend events about the chicken farming business, and chat to as many people as you can, because this is how you'll learn tips, tricks, and advice, and meet prospective customers. Also, make good use of social media to let people know about your business. For example, create a Facebook page for your business, running a Twitter account can be worth a try too. The more images you can use on social media, the more effective this is, as people engage with images more than words. You can get business cards with your logo and contact details printed on, and hand them out whenever you speak with people so that they have a way to remember and contact you.

Egg Sale Business

If you've decided that egg sales will be a key part of your business, you next need to find out if there is actually a market for freshly laid chicken eggs in the area that you live. I'd be very surprised if there wasn't because they're such a versatile ingredient in cooking, for use on their own, or in baking. But you need to know the market well. You need to know how much other people are selling eggs for, and whether their eggs are any different from yours. Are their chickens fed organic feed? Are the chickens pastured free range? Next, you'll need to think about where you will take your eggs. Will this be at local stores? Will you sell them from your garden, at a farm shop, or at a farmers' market? If you're only selling a small number of eggs, the laws in your area may allow this (but be sure to do thorough research), but if you really want to scale up big time, then you may need to have a USDA-inspected egg washing facility. Most places are keen to have a fresh supply of eggs, but if you live in a very small rural area, it could be that there's already too many supplied. The benefits of selling locally are that you don't have to travel far, and this can reduce costs and time, and selling locally you will get a loyal customer base who know you.

It is super important to be fully clued up on the laws about selling eggs. The laws in your area may or may not allow you to recycle egg cartons. If you suggest your eggs are organic, you may need to prove this and fully meet organic standards. In order to check your laws, you could ask a county extension agent, state poultry, or agriculture specialist about laws and any permits you may require.

Take time to put together a business plan that identifies your market and looks at future growth if you decide to expand your business. You will need to look at costs both for what money you have spent on chickens, their accommodation, food, healthcare, time spent looking after them, and realistically at what you need to be selling in order to generate a profit, and how long it will take to achieve. You can use your business plan to then make informed decisions about how many chickens you require to make the number of eggs you need to make a profit.

For example, if you want to sell 120 eggs per week, then you would probably need 25 to 30 chickens to create this quantity of eggs. Ensure that you have adequate space for the chickens, can afford to look after them well, and that you could realistically sell this number of eggs. How many eggs you think you can sell will also help you decide how much to charge for them. Do remember that over time you will need to keep on making improvements to your chicken coop areas and fencing, as well as pay the vet bills, so allow for these things when you're pricing and anticipating profit. There are always unexpected expenses that crop up in businesses. When thinking about prices of keeping chickens and prices of eggs, think about how much chicken feed you use, their treats, water, supplements, bedding, power, cost of cartons, labels, fuel (if needed) to get the eggs to market, and so on. This will help you price your eggs accordingly. In the US, it is estimated that the average person eats approximately 260 eggs per year, so there is definitely a market for them. Egg prices vary, and typically cost $3 for a dozen, and $4 for 18.

You can look back at earlier chapters of this book, to have a reminder about good breeds of chickens for egg laying, and where to purchase them from, and how to take care of everything regarding them. You'll need to consider the climate you live in for types of breeds too.

Chapter 8 on Egg Production covers cleaning and storing eggs, but this is especially important if you are selling to others, so make sure you clean them carefully and reduce the risk of something like salmonella poisoning.

As a part of your business plan, you can think about your packaging for eggs, and the type of label you want to use, your logo, and other information. Do ensure that you follow all local and state laws regarding packaging and selling eggs. You may find that a lot of your customers come from word-of-mouth advertising. People tell their family and friends, and your customer base can increase dramatically. You could consider flyers as a fairly cheap way to advertise, and put them through doors locally.

When your business is running along happily, it is worth taking time aside every now and then to assess and evaluate the business. There will always be things that could be more productive, and run more efficiently, or work in a different way. Always check that you're happy working in the egg sale business too. Of course, everyone will have bad days, but this is a career choice that you should enjoy, and it should help to contribute to a happy and sustainable lifestyle for you.

Some of your customers may want different colored eggs, so if this is the case, you could add Araucanas to your flock for blue eggs, or some Easter-Egger chickens who lay different colored eggs.

It's perhaps an obvious point to make, but it can make good business sense to plough back as much of the money as possible back into the business to ensure that the chickens are paying for their upkeep and a little more.

You may find your egg selling business goes from strength to strength, so over time you may need to extend the coop and give the chickens more land to roam on, and you'll need to increase the number of chickens you have too.

Do keep in mind that initially you may not make any profit from selling your eggs because you will have major initial expenses, such as buying the chickens, the coop, fencing, and feed, but over time you will start to get money in, and depending on how many eggs you sell, this can soon build up.

If you're starting out small and aren't ready to increase your flock just yet, but would like to make some small income from eggs that your family is unable to consume, you could put a "fresh farm eggs" sign on your drive. You can use an "honor stand" where people can take eggs and honestly pay you for them without you needing to be there. You could create a client list and deliver eggs to them frequently. You could go to a farmer's market or ask local stores if they would like to sell any of your eggs.

Chicken Broiler Business

If you wish to raise chickens for meat and breed chickens for this, the chickens are known as broilers. It is a good idea to start out by making a business plan which includes your goals, and your route to achieve them. You again need to ensure that there is a market for meat. You'll need to consider the basics if you don't already have these, such as land, capital, and equipment. You'll need space for buildings, space for land to grow crops, and equipment and machinery to keep things running smoothly. It is only worth starting a broiler business if you have broiler companies in your area who want to buy from you. It is best to set up these contacts at first, rather than doing it the other way round.

You may want to breed chickens for meat or have a business of incubating eggs and raising chicks. You can sell day-old chicks to bigger producers. This hopefully goes without saying, but do your research and invest in training if you are interested in rearing chicks and haven't done so before because if you don't know what you're doing, these are chicks' lives at stake.

You can decide whether you want chickens for meat, eggs, chicks, or all three. You could start out with 4–10 birds initially and grow from there over time as demand grows. As well as relying on word-of-mouth advertising to let people know what chicken product you're selling, you can also use online classified websites for marketing.

If you have scaled up your broiler or chick rearing business, then feed will be one of your biggest costs for them. It is advisable to buy feed directly from suppliers and manufacturers so that you can avoid markup costs that are incurred from buying via an intermediary agent who is looking to make their own profit from the product. Buying in bulk will save you in the long term. If you have land, you could consider replacing some of the commercial feed for broilers with cracked grains that you grow yourself.

If you are raising chickens for meat, you need to decide whether they're sold alive per bird or by weight. If you sell via someone like an abattoir, you'll again lose some profit, but if you don't do this, you will need to process the birds yourself in terms of culling, plucking, and eviscerating them. In your initial business plan, you should consider your approach to this, and do plenty of research into what is more

worthwhile to you. Anything you do yourself may appear to have financial savings, but it will cost in time and labor.

Keeping broilers healthy is essential to keep your business running well, it can be helpful to ensure all your birds are vaccinated to prevent health issues, and if there's ever any sign of illness, get your birds to a vet as soon as possible to get this sorted and prevent it from spreading.

When we first started out with our chickens, initially we used them to lay eggs just for our family. When we reached a point where we had more than we could use, we gave them away to family and friends, and our neighbors. People really loved the eggs, and started asking us for them, and offering to give us some money for them. This soon developed into regular weekly orders, and then requests came from their family and friends, all via word-of-mouth. We would sometimes set up a stand on our driveway with an honesty box too, and we found that people were typically honest and trustworthy. We figured that if eggs ever disappeared and weren't accounted for financially, that it was probably that people didn't have the money on them and would drop it in at a later date. If ever they were taken out of genuine necessity, then they'd be welcome to them anyhow. We increased our egg-laying flock over time and produced so many eggs we would take them to sell at a local farmers' market. We also sold produce that was made using the eggs, such as quiches and cakes. They have genuinely created more profit for us than cost, and they help us to live a more sustainable lifestyle.

Key takeaways from this chapter:

1. Chickens are versatile to create a business from: you can use them for meat, eggs, to breed chicks, to make manure, or all of these.

2. Before you get started, check the laws in your area or state regarding selling chicken eggs, meat, or chicks, and also check what permits you may need.

3. It's a great idea to make a detailed business plan before starting your business.

4. Carefully contemplate the market to sell to.

5. Create a webpage, logo, and packaging.

6. Network with others in the business.

7. Use social media to advertise your products.

8. Consider a niche, this could be if your chicken products are organic or pasture fed.

9. Think about where you will sell your chicken products: on your driveway with an honor box, a farmers' market, local stores, or a client list that you deliver to.

10. Try to account for all costs when you're creating a business plan prior to starting the business and think of unexpected costs too.

11. Select relevant breeds for the purpose you want the chickens for.

12. Consider how you'll advertise, this could be through word-of-mouth, flyers, classifieds, or social media.

13. If you want to sell broilers, try to ensure that you know of companies locally who will buy the broilers from you before you even start your business.

14. Do your research and consider getting training so that you know what you're doing with the chickens.

15. Start small and grow the business gradually.

16. You could try to cut down on feed costs by growing your own if you have the land available for this.

17. Get your chickens vaccinated and get them to the vet swiftly if they ever look ill.

Conclusion

The chickens we have most definitely enriched our lives. We have a wonderful cycle of new chicks being born which is adorable to see. Each of our chickens have their own distinct personalities, which is funny and amusing. They are friendly creatures and a pleasure to have around. Our chickens provide us with a wonderful supply of fresh eggs for our own use to eat and bake with, and we make an income from the abundance of eggs we receive selling them locally. The chickens help to keep our land pest-free and help with gardening. Their poop creates incredible compost, which is fantastic to grow vegetables and plants in, and it enriches our soil with essential nutrients. Chickens help us to live a sustainable lifestyle and for that we're very grateful.

I hope that this book has given you a good grounding in things that you need to contemplate before raising chickens. I hope it has taken you through your options whether you want chickens for eggs, meat, or to breed chicks. This book is aimed at beginners to give you a guide to breeds, information about the housing they require, the facilities they need, how to feed them, how to care for their health, and information about eggs and meat. It should be viewed as a one-stop-shop for everything a beginner needs to know about chickens.

From reading the book, you should have a good idea of the benefits of chickens, things you need to consider before embarking on the journey of raising chickens, how to select the right breed for the purposes you want, whether that is to lay eggs, produce meat, or to breed chicks. You will have a better understanding of where you can purchase chickens from, and how many is a good number to start off with for a beginner.

You will know the various options you have for chicken housing and runs, and whether you decide to purchase these or have a go at building them yourself. You should think carefully about the size, location, insulation, and ventilation of shelter for chickens.

You will know what to feed chickens depending on their purpose and age. You will have a good idea of health care for chickens with an awareness of common health issues to watch out for, as well as tips to keep your chickens at the peak of health.

The book breaks down activities you can expect to be involved in if you choose to have chickens, such as things you'll do daily, weekly, monthly, and semi-yearly, which will allow you to build a routine, which can be really helpful to someone who is new to raising chickens so that you know you're covering everything you need to.

If you wish to breed chickens, you'll learn about how to mate them, and whether to incubate eggs using an incubator or with the help of a broody hen, and how to raise chicks.

Chapter 8 is one of my favorite chapters, about egg production, and looking at identifying laying hens, why hens may not lay and how you can help encourage them to, how to gather, store, and clean eggs, how to check them for quality, and interestingly how you can preserve fresh (not boiled or pickled) eggs for 8 months and possibly up to 2 years!

You will learn about raising chickens for meat which are known as broilers, how to feed them, health issues that can occur, and about when and how to humanely butcher them, and how to store poultry.

Chapter 10 is another of my favorite chapters, about making really good use of your chickens in the garden. You can get chickens involved in all manner of gardening work, from pest control to tilling, weeding, as well as them helping to produce incredible compost!

The final chapter of the book gives you plenty of food for thought whether you'd like to turn your chicken produce into an actual business, and the first steps you'd need to consider with that, from checking local laws to creating a detailed business plan, considering costs, marketing/advertising, and so on.

So, you've reached the end of the book, my key bit of advice now is to go forth and raise chickens! Trust me, it'll be one of the best decisions you make. Remember to research the laws in your area thoroughly, consider what purpose you want them for, look into breeds, and get everything in place before you start. Start small and gradually increase your flock over time. Be warned though—raising chickens is addictive!

Resources

Organizations

American Bantam Association

https://www.bantamclub.com

American Pastured Poultry Producers Association

https://apppa.org

American Poultry Association

https://amerpoultryassn.com

National Chicken Council

https://www.nationalchickencouncil.org

Poultry Organizations

https://www.communitychickens.com/poultry-organizations-zw02103ztil/

U.S. Poultry & Egg Association

https://www.uspoultry.org

Can You Raise Chickens in Your Area?

Backyard Poultry. 2021. Can I Raise Chickens in My Area? 8th August 2021. Online.

https://backyardpoultry.iamcountryside.com/chickens-101/can-i-raise-chickens-in-my-area/

My Pet Chicken. 2021. Chicken Help. *My Pet Chicken*. Online.

https://www.mypetchicken.com/backyard-chickens/chicken-help/How-do-I-figure-out-whether-or-not-Im-allowed-to-H212.aspx

Schwartz, Daniel Mark. 2020. Are Chickens Allowed in Your City? How to Find Out What's Allowed. *Off Grid Permaculture*. Online.

https://offgridpermaculture.com/Beginners/Are_Chickens_Allowed_in_Your_City__How_To_Find_Out_What_s_Allowed.html

Breed Information

Backyard Poultry. 2021. 3 of The Best Dual-Purpose Chicken Breeds. 29th November 2021. Online.

https://backyardpoultry.iamcountryside.com/chickens-101/3-of-the-best-dual-purpose-chicken-breeds/

Happy Chicken, 2021. Best Meat Chicken Breeds. November 18th, 2021. Online.

https://www.thehappychickencoop.com/best-meat-chicken-breeds/

Morning Chores. 2021. How to Go about Choosing the Perfect Chicken Breeds for You. *Morning Chores*. Online.

https://morningchores.com/choosing-a-chicken-breed/

Morning Chores. 2021. 10 Best Chicken Breeds for Meat (and Dual-Purpose) to Raise in Your Backyard. *Morning Chores*. Online.

https://morningchores.com/meat-chickens/

Morning Chores. 2021. Top 10 Chicken Breeds That Will Give You up to 300 Eggs per Year. *Morning Chores*. Online.

https://morningchores.com/egg-laying-chickens/

Roy's Farm. 2021. Best Guide for Choosing a Chicken Breed for Beginners. *Roy's Farm*. 16th October 2021. Online.

https://www.roysfarm.com/choosing-a-chicken-breed/

Steele, Lisa. 2021. Raising Chickens 101: Choosing the Right Chicken Breeds. *The Old Farmer's Almanac*. 2nd March 2021. Online.

https://www.almanac.com/raising-chickens-101-choosing-chicken-breeds

The Happy Chicken Coop. 2021. 10 Chicken Breeds That Will Lay Lots of Eggs for You. 6th March 2021, Online.

https://www.thehappychickencoop.com/10-breeds-of-chicken-that-will-lay-lots-of-eggs-for-you/

The Happy Chicken Coop. 2021. Best Chickens for Eggs and Meat: Dual Purpose Chickens. 16th November 2021, Online.

https://www.thehappychickencoop.com/best-chickens-for-eggs-and-meat/

Chicken Housing

Andrews, Cath. 2021. Chicken runs: how to make sure they suit your flock's needs. *Raising Happy Chickens*. Online.

https://www.raising-happy-chickens.com/chicken-runs.html

Cowan, Shannon. 2016. Housing Your Backyard Chickens. 24th May 2016. Online.

https://learn.eartheasy.com/articles/housing-your-backyard-chickens/

Dakota Storage Buildings. 2021. Should you Buy or DIT Your First Backyard Chicken Coop? June 17th 2021. Online.

https://www.dakotastorage.com/blog/should-you-buy-or-diy-your-first-backyard-chicken-coop

Happy Chicken. 2019. Chicken Fencing – Which One Should You Choose? *The Happy Chicken Coop*. 11th November 2019. Online.

https://www.thehappychickencoop.com/chicken-fencing/

Morning Chores. 2021. Housing Your Chickens: All You Need to Know to Do It Properly. *Morning Chores*. Online.

https://morningchores.com/chicken-housing/

Robert. 2021. Chicken Coop Design Considerations: Rules for a Happy Hen House. *Chicken Coop Design Plans*. 18th April 2021. Online.

https://coopdesignplans.com/design-rules-for-happy-hens/

Winger, Jill. 2020. How to Build a Chicken Run. *The Prairie Homestead*. Online. 19th September 2020.

https://www.theprairiehomestead.com/2016/08/build-chicken-run.html

Feeding Chickens

Arcuri, Lauren. 2021. Watering Backyard Chickens. *The Spruce*. 21st June 2021. Online.

https://www.thespruce.com/water-your-chickens-3016561

Gennetta, Nicole. 2021. The Ultimate list of what chickens can and cannot eat. *Heritage Acres Market.* 13th December 2020, updated May 22nd 2021. Online. https://www.heritageacresmarket.com/what-chickens-can-and-cant-eat/

Smith, Kassandra. 2020. All the Different Types of Chicken Feed Explained. 26th June, 2020. Online. https://www.backyardchickencoops.com.au/blogs/learning-centre/all-the-different-types-of-chicken-feed-explained

The Happy Chicken Coop. 2021. 7 Surprising Rules for Feeding Chickens. 1st March 2021, Online. https://www.thehappychickencoop.com/7-surprising-rules-for-feeding-chickens/

Health Care

Andrews, Cath. 2021. Biosecurity: how to keep your chickens safe. *Raising Happy Chickens.* Online. https://www.raising-happy-chickens.com/biosecurity-and-chickens.html

Freedom Ranger Hatchery. 2021. How to Prevent and Treat the 5 Most Common Chicken Diseases. Online. https://www.freedomrangerhatchery.com/blog/how-to-prevent-and-treat-the-5-most-common-chicken-diseases/

Mississippi State University Extension. 2021. Diseases of Poultry. Online. https://extension.msstate.edu/agriculture/livestock/poultry/diseases-poultry

Mormino, Kathy Shea. 2021. Biosecurity for Backyard Chickens. *The Chicken Chick.* Online.

https://the-chicken-chick.com/biosecurity-for-backyard-chickens/

Morning Chores. 2021. 13 Common Chicken Diseases Every Chicken Keeper Should Know About (and How to Treat Them). *Morning Chores.* Online.

https://morningchores.com/chicken-diseases/

MSD Veterinary Manual. 2021. Common Infectious Diseases in Backyard Poultry. Online.

https://www.msdvetmanual.com/exotic-and-laboratory-animals/backyard-poultry/common-infectious-diseases-in-backyard-poultry

The Happy Chicken Coop. 2021. The Complete Guide to Chicken Parasites. 17th November 2019, Online.

https://www.thehappychickencoop.com/guide-to-chicken-parasites/

Routine Management

Arcuri, Lauren. 2021. Easy Chicken Care Tasks to Make Part of Your Routine. 20th May 2021. Online.

https://www.thespruce.com/daily-and-monthly-chicken-care-tasks-3016823

Keeping Chickens UK. 2021. Daily Chicken Care Routine. *Keeping Chickens UK.* Online.

https://www.keepingchickensuk.co.uk/daily-chicken-care/

Steele, Lisa. 2017. Top tips for keeping chickens when you work all day. *Fresh Eggs Daily*. Online.

https://www.fresheggsdaily.blog/2017/01/my-top-tips-for-keeping-chickens-when.html

Breeding Chickens

Almanac. 2021. Raising chickens 101: How to Raise Baby Chickens. Online.

https://www.almanac.com/raising-chickens-101-how-raise-baby-chickens

Mile Four. N.d. How to Breed Chickens/Ultimate Guide. *Mile Four*. Online.

https://milefour.com/blogs/learn/how-to-breed-chickens#3

Omlet. 2018. Breeding Chickens. Online

https://www.omlet.co.uk/guide/chickens/chicken_care/breeding_chickens/

Egg production

Arcuri, Lauren. 2020. Collecting and Cleaning Chicken Eggs. *The Spruce*. 21st July 2020. Online.

https://www.thespruce.com/collect-clean-and-store-chicken-eggs-3016828

Belanger, Jd. 2020. Everything worth knowing about chicken eggs. *Backyard Poultry*. 14th March 2020. Online.

https://backyardpoultry.iamcountryside.com/eggs-meat/everything-worth-knowing-about-chicken-eggs/

Jacob, Jacquie. N.d. Raising Chickens for Egg Production. *Extension*. Online.

https://poultry.extension.org/articles/poultry-management/raising-chickens-for-egg-production/

Stregowski, Jenna. 2021. Can chickens lay eggs without a rooster? *The Spruce*. Online. 24th November 2021.

https://www.thespruce.com/can-hens-lay-eggs-without-roosters-3385618

Thomas, Carolyn. 2020. Preserved Eggs – Water Glassing Eggs for Long-Term Storage. *HomesteadingFamily*. 29th January 2020. Online.

https://homesteadingfamily.com/preserved-eggs-water-glassing-eggs-for-long-term-storage/

Meat Production

Happy Chicken. 2021. Chicken Processing: Know when to Slaughter your Chickens. 27th July, 2021. *Happy Chicken*. Online.

https://www.thehappychickencoop.com/chicken-processing-know-when-to-slaughter-your-chickens/

Happy Chicken. 2020. How to Raise Meat Chickens. *The Happy Chicken Coop*. Online.

https://www.thehappychickencoop.com/how-to-raise-meat-chickens/

Heather. 2020. How to raise chickens for meat on the homestead. *The Homesteading Hippy*. Online.

https://thehomesteadinghippy.com/raising-chickens-meat/

Poindexter, Jennifer. 2021. How to Butcher a Chicken: 7 Steps to Humanely Kill, Pluck, and Clean Your Chickens. *Morning Chores*. Online.

https://morningchores.com/how-to-butcher-a-chicken/

Ussery, Harvey and Ellen. 2005. Homestead Poultry Butchering: Afterwards. *The Modern Homestead.* Online.

https://www.themodernhomestead.us/article/Butchering-Afterwards.html

Composting and Using Chicken Manure

Duncan, Judy. 2005. Composting Chicken Manure. *Tilth Alliance.* Online.

http://www.tilthalliance.org/learn/resources-1/city-chickens/compostingchickenmanure

Extension. N.d. Using chicken manure safely in home gardens and landscapes. University of Nevada, Reno. *Extension.* Online.

https://extension.unr.edu/publication.aspx?PubID=3028

Rhoades, Heather. 2021. Using Chicken Manure Fertilizer in Your Garden. *Gardening Know How.* Online. 18th June 2021.

https://www.gardeningknowhow.com/composting/manures/chicken-manure-fertilizer.htm

Putting Chickens to Work in the Garden

Elaine B. 2014. Put Your Chickens to Work in Your Garden! *Scoop from the Coop.* 21st May 2014. Online.

https://www.scoopfromthecoop.com/put-your-chickens-to-work-in-your-garden/

Kelsey. 2020. How to Put Chickens to Work in the Garden. *Green Willow Homestead.* 1st September 2020. Online.

https://www.greenwillowhomestead.com/blog/how-to-put-chickens-to-work-in-the-garden

Knerl, Linsey. 2019. Chickens in the Garden: What you need to Know. 8th February 2019. Online. *Gardener's Path*.

https://gardenerspath.com/how-to/animals-and-wildlife/chickens-help-garden/

Maynard, Pam. 2021. Raising Chickens and Poultry for Home Pest Control. *Grit*. Online.

https://www.grit.com/farm-and-garden/raising-chickens-and-poultry-for-home-pest-control/

Pleasant, Barbara. 2021. Gardening With Chickens for Fantastic Natural Pest Control. *Mother Earth News*. Online.

https://www.motherearthnews.com/organic-gardening/pest-control/gardening-with-chickens-pest-control-zw0z1304zkin

Winger, Jill. 2018. 8 Ways to Use Chickens in the Garden. *The Prairie Homestead*. Online. 17th March 2018.

https://www.theprairiehomestead.com/2015/02/chickens-in-the-garden.html

Chicken Farm Business

Arcuri, Lauren. 2021. How to Start an Egg Business. *Treehugger*. Online. 14th July, 2021.

https://www.treehugger.com/start-an-egg-business-3016906

Ray, Henna. 2021. 20 Rules for Staring Your Own Poultry Farm. *Design Hill*. 20th August 2021. Online.

https://www.designhill.com/design-blog/rules-for-starting-your-own-poultry-farm/

Roy's Farm. 2021. How to Start Chicken Farming Business Easily. *Roy's Farm*. Online.

https://www.roysfarm.com/start-chicken-farming-business/

The Hen House Collection. 2021. How much does it cost to raise chickens? *The Hen House Collection*. Online.

https://www.thehenhousecollection.com/blog/cost-to-raise-chickens/

Uitert, Maat van. 2020. How much does it cost to own a chicken? Egg cost comparison. *The Frugal Chicken*. 26th September 2020. Online.

https://thefrugalchicken.com/how-much-does-it-cost-own-a-chicken/

Van Eeden, Dona. 2021. How to start your own chicken farm. *Food for Mzansi*. 11th May 2021. Online.

https://www.foodformzansi.co.za/start-your-own-chicken-farm/

Wilson, Wendy Bedwell. 2011. Start a Successful Egg Business That Makes You Money. Online. *Hobby Farms.*

https://www.hobbyfarms.com/start-a-successful-egg-business-that-makes-you-money-3/

Index

Printed in Great Britain
by Amazon

24321777R00106